The Object Less[on]
to magic: the b[...]
and animate th[...]
political strug[gle...]
Filled with fas[...]
accessible prose, the books [...]
come to life. Be warned: once you've read a few of these,
you'll start walking around your house, picking up
random objects, and musing aloud: 'I wonder what the
story is behind this thing?'"

Steven Johnson, author of *Where Good Ideas
Come From* and *How We Got to Now*

Object Lessons describes themselves as 'short, beautiful
books,' and to that, I'll say, amen. . . . If you read enough
Object Lessons books, you'll fill your head with plenty
of trivia to amaze and annoy your friends and loved
ones—caution recommended on pontificating on the
objects surrounding you. More importantly, though. . .
they inspire us to take a second look at parts of the
everyday that we've taken for granted. These are not
so much lessons about the objects themselves, but
opportunities for self-reflection and storytelling. They
remind us that we are surrounded by a wondrous
world, as long as we care to look."

John Warner, *The Chicago Tribune*

"Besides being beautiful little hand-sized objects themselves, showcasing exceptional writing, the wonder of these books is that they exist at all . . . Uniformly excellent, engaging, thought-provoking, and informative."

Jennifer Bort Yacovissi, *Washington Independent Review of Books*

". . . edifying and entertaining . . . perfect for slipping in a pocket and pulling out when life is on hold."

Sarah Murdoch, *Toronto Star*

"For my money, Object Lessons is the most consistently interesting nonfiction book series in America."

Megan Volpert, *PopMatters*

"Though short, at roughly 25,000 words apiece, these books are anything but slight."

Marina Benjamin, *New Statesman*

"[W]itty, thought-provoking, and poetic . . . These little books are a page-flipper's dream."

John Timpane, *The Philadelphia Inquirer*

The joy of the series, of reading *Remote Control, Golf Ball, Driver's License, Drone, Silence, Glass, Refrigerator, Hotel,* and *Waste* (more titles are listed as forthcoming) in quick succession, lies in encountering the various turns through which each of their authors has been put by his or her object. As for Benjamin, so for the authors of the series, the object predominates, sits squarely center stage, directs the action. The object decides the genre, the chronology, and the limits of the study. Accordingly, the author has to take her cue from the *thing* she chose or that chose her. The result is a wonderfully uneven series of books, each one a *thing* unto itself."

Julian Yates, *Los Angeles Review of Books*

The Object Lessons series has a beautifully simple premise. Each book or essay centers on a specific object. This can be mundane or unexpected, humorous or politically timely. Whatever the subject, these descriptions reveal the rich worlds hidden under the surface of things."

Christine Ro, *Book Riot*

. . . a sensibility somewhere between Roland Barthes and Wes Anderson."

Simon Reynolds, author of *Retromania: Pop Culture's Addiction to Its Own Past*

My favourite series of short pop culture books"

Zoomer magazine

OBJECT LESSONS

A book series about the hidden lives of ordinary things.

Series Editors:

Ian Bogost and Christopher Schaberg

In association with

Program *in* Public Scholarship

Washington University in St.Louis

BOOKS IN THE SERIES

Swimming Pool

PIOTR FLORCZYK

BLOOMSBURY ACADEMIC
NEW YORK · LONDON · OXFORD · NEW DELHI · SYDNEY

BLOOMSBURY ACADEMIC
Bloomsbury Publishing Inc
1385 Broadway, New York, NY 10018, USA
50 Bedford Square, London, WC1B 3DP, UK
29 Earlsfort Terrace, Dublin 2, Ireland

First published in the United States of America 2024

Cover design: Alice Marwick

Library of Congress Cataloging-in-Publication Data
Names: Florczyk, Piotr, author.
Title: Swimming pool / Piotr Florczyk.
Description: New York: Bloomsbury Academic, 2024. | Series: Object Lessons |
Includes bibliographical references and index. | Summary: "A blend of personal
narrative and critical inquiry, Swimming Pool explores the swimming pool as a symbol
of status, athleticism, suburbia, and artistic pursuit"– Provided by publisher.
Identifiers: LCCN 2023025739 (print) | LCCN 2023025740 (ebook) |
ISBN 9781501394874 (PB) | ISBN 9781501394881 (eBook) |
ISBN 9781501394898 (ePDF) | ISBN 9781501394904 (other)
Subjects: LCSH: Swimming pools. | Swimming.
Classification: LCC GV838.53.S85 F56 2024 (print) | LCC GV838.53.S85 (ebook) |
DDC 797.2–dc23/eng/20230828
LC record available at https://lccn.loc.gov/2023025739
LC ebook record available at https://lccn.loc.gov/2023025740

ISBN: PB: 978-1-5013-9487-4
ePDF: 978-1-5013-9489-8
eBook: 978-1-5013-9488-1

Series: Object Lessons

Typeset by Deanta Global Publishing Services, Chennai, India
Printed and bound in Great Britain

To find out more about our authors and books visit www.bloomsbury.com and
sign up for our newsletters.

CONTENTS

1 WHERE DO YOU SWIM?

I can't tell anymore where I was on Thursday, March 19, 2020, but I am sure my day did not begin with a swim workout at the Culver City municipal pool, aka the Plunge. Typically, I would've been there at 5:30 a.m., to coach or swim for an hour. The outdoor facility, which opened in 1949, can be set up for either short course (25 yards) or long course (50 meters), with the latter a particular draw for serious swimmers who believe, not without some justification, that one gets a better workout swimming long course, where there are fewer turns and thus opportunities to rest between each lap. Or perhaps it's the fact that swimming events at the Olympics are conducted in a 50-meter pool, and who wouldn't want to be as fast as those chiseled stars? That morning the pool would've been set up for long course.

If anyone did show up to swim at the crack of dawn on that day, it's because they hadn't heard that Eric Garcetti's "Safer at Home" order had gone into effect, consequently shutting down all public pools in Los Angeles County. To stem the rise of Covid-19 cases, drastic actions by public officials had been expected, but few thought that outdoor fitness facilities were going to be affected. Exercising— swimming or water-jogging or dancing to the music in an aquarobics class—seemed safe compared to huffing and puffing in a poorly ventilated gym. Of course, swimmers pass each other in the water, breathing in and out, and sometimes even chitchat at the walls or on deck, but in the grand scheme of things those moments do not last very long. Just close the locker rooms and let us swim, I heard my friends say. After public health officials began to acknowledge a correlation between Covid-19 deaths and obesity, the voices of those calling for outdoor pools to remain open became harder to silence.

Following the shutdown, many swimmers began to venture into the cold Pacific to get their yards in, even though swimming dressed in a wetsuit, no matter how much the materials and design have improved from the days when wetsuits resembled—and felt like—straitjackets, isn't everyone's cup of tea. Additionally, some swimmers are wedded to the black line they follow on the bottom of the pool, and the lane lines that help them swim straight, and thus find the open space of the ocean frustrating—and scary; running unexpectedly into a piece of loose kelp can be very frightening indeed. Still, in no time displaced pool swimmers began to organize themselves into packs that would swim together in the ocean at all times of the day, including in early mornings. "Isn't that shark feeding time?" I'd ask only half-jokingly after being invited to come out for one of these swims off Santa Monica or Hermosa Beach.

Still others turned to their attention to backyard pools. Anybody who has flown into LAX knows that there is no shortage of backyard pools in the LA area, although most of them are either too short or too shallow—or have curved walls that make flip turns impractical or outright dangerous. To make swimming in a tiny pool more challenging, bungy cords and similar contraptions were devised and implemented, allowing the swimmer to get a workout while swimming in place. Dedicated lap swimmers used to turn their noses up at those so-called endless pools that resembled rectangular jacuzzies, even though the company making them employed Michael Phelps to advertise their products, but now they had no choice than to embrace them. Some even placed a large mirror at the bottom of the pool, ostensibly to help them correct their technique and not just to stare at themselves.

Thus, it was with joy that my wife and I, along with several others, accepted an invitation from a friend to start swimming in his private 10-by-60-foot pool. He lives in the Pacific Palisades area of Los Angeles, in a house perched on a hillside overlooking Santa Monica Bay. "How many tons of concrete did it take to build this thing?" I wondered when I saw the pool for the first time. Designed by a local company, the pool, whose deepest point measures 10 ft and its shallowest 3.5 ft, is situated in the lower part of a slopping lot, with the house overlooking it; I imagined someone diving or rather jumping into it from the terrace above. Nine caissons—each 3 ft in diameter and going down 20 ft—secure the pool firmly to the hillside. The pool's north side has a retaining wall, and the south side sits above ground. The construction took three months.

Truth be told, I used to question why people needed backyard pools if they lived, like my friend, near the beach. No pool, even if it's filled with saltwater, can duplicate the feeling and experience of swimming in the ocean, where waves and currents are the main attraction. On the other hand, a backyard pool can arguably extend the experience of living near the coast, which many people find synonymous with alternating between playing in the sun and cooling off in the water. In other words, the pool is an extension of

FIGURE 1 Photo by Piotr Florczyk.

beach culture—even in Southern California, where the brisk water temps keep many people of out the surf—rather than a substitute for it.

With a decent size deck and a jacuzzi, my friend's pool could be just that—a place to sunbathe and have lunch—but its shape and dimensions suggest the pool was constructed for lap-swimming. At 20 yards in length and almost 3.5 yards across, the pool is a skinny rectangle, which means a swimmer could, after slightly adopting his sets meant for a short-course pool, do a proper workout in it. What's more, this pool matches the façade of the house, laid out as it is in materials much darker in color than the light blue or white most of us associate with backyard pools. The darker bottom makes the pool feel much deeper than it is, which is a key aspect of replicating the experience of swimming in a regular-size swimming pool. Because the turbulence produced by a body moving through water is much more noticeable in a shallow pool, where the waves produced bounce off the walls and the bottom with a great frequency, a shallow pool can not only feel claustrophobic, but also slow the swimmer down. My friend, who holds multiple world-records as a masters swimmer, would know the difference.

Moreover, while his pool is surrounded by lush vegetation, like the rest of the property and the hillside itself, its shape creates a contrast between it and the stunning landscape, with the curving Santa Monica Bay as its highlight. Indeed, the pool's straight lines accentuate its secondary role, that is, that of yet another observation deck, if you will, offering unencumbered views of the city of Santa Monica to the south and parts of Malibu to the north. On the mornings when fog shrouds the area and then burns off, retreating over the ocean, only to come back in several times throughout the day, the swimmer can feel at one with his surroundings.

When public health officials in Los Angeles began to ease the restrictions meant to control the spread of the virus, the swimming community was ecstatic, although it soon became clear that not everyone would be allowed to swim in their favorite public pool. For one, not all public facilities reopened. Second, those that did, like the Culver City Plunge, severely limited the number of swimmers allowed to enter the facility at any given time. Furthermore, an elaborate online reservation system was put in place, limiting the access to each of the pool's lanes to a single swimmer. I remember queuing outside one of the pools, then having my vaccination card examined and my temperature taken before I was allowed to go in, with the understanding that the locker room remained closed and that I wouldn't be able to shower afterwards. People did what they could to ensure that, no matter their allergen tolerance levels, they would not sneeze anywhere near the front entrance. Once in, I looked across the twenty-plus lanes and saw two dozen swimmers, which paled in comparison to the 60-70 I would see pre-pandemic. Swimming may be the activity for introverts, but the sight of the pool being almost empty despite being open made my heart heavy.

Some swimmers never returned to the pool. Having switched to swimming in the ocean, they found the new entry regulations too much to bear. The restrictions continued to ease though, with the next stage consisting of allowing 4-6 swimmers per lane during organized masters team workouts. Congregating at the wall, however, was not allowed, which meant that the last swimmer in each lane, when it was time to stop and rest, had to hold on to the lane line at least several yards out from the wall. To decrease chances for close-contact and interaction, half of the swimmers had to start from the opposite side. This created quite the stir, because not only did it suggest that up to six swimmers passing each other every single lap was acceptable and safe, but it also meant that everyone had to slow down, so that the pack that started at one end would not run into the tail end of the pack that started at the other end. To prevent the packs from having to pass each other, training sets had to be modified, which translated into a lot of 25s and 50s. No wonder the ocean swimmers, many of whom participate in open-water races that average several miles in length and thus require a more endurance-oriented training, stayed away from the pools.

What about the rest of the populace? Sadly, those who had been planning on finally taking swim lessons or enrolling their children in a swim program missed out on the ability to do so, which might've discouraged them from ever learning how to swim. On the other hand, I would imagine that some well-to-do homeowners and homeowners' associations elected to build a pool for themselves or their communities.

This would explain, at least in part, the more than doubling of the stock price of Pool Corp., a major pool building and maintenance company, between March and November of 2020.[1]

The above-ground pool, for instance, is a common sight in the parts of the country with colder climates. Honeoye Falls, New York, is a village south of the city of Rochester. Like much of Western New York State, the area is well-known for its snowy winters and short summers. Which does not stop homeowners from investing in pools. Due to the laws of physics—that is, something called hydrostatic pressure—pools, especially in-ground pools, should not be emptied of water unless it is necessary to do so, since an in-ground pool without water in it will succumb to the pressure of the groundwater pushing up against the bottom and the sides, leading to major structural damage. With an above-ground pool it is also necessary to maintain water in it, but mainly to make sure that the pool, which is often round, doesn't collapse on itself.

The pool in the picture seems well-maintained, with a proper filtration system keeping it safe and free of algae. A tarp made of what looks like polyethylene is placed over it to keep the water temperature stable. The ladder helps the bathers come in and out with ease. Anyone expecting a proper deck space, as is customary for most suburban backyard pools, might find this pool out of place just sitting there in a middle of a lawn, next to towering trees, which in turn provide a much-needed shade to anyone frolicking in

FIGURE 2 Photo by G. Lofthus.

the pool on muggy days. Nevertheless, the owners have done a nice job of making sure the pool does not feel disconnected from the property, and I can imagine an archway entrance and a stone path leading up to the pool, suggesting an adventure awaiting anyone crossing the threshold. The pool is too shallow for diving, so no chance for a diving board to be installed, but it isn't hard to picture oneself playing in it with a beach ball or just floating, drink in hand, on a tube. In fact, a family floating on tubes could organize themselves into an aquatic version of bumper cars.

The bumper cars metaphor for swimmers floating around in innertubes, on inflatable mattresses and the so-called noodles, bouncing off each other not unlike kids chasing a ball or playing tag, isn't as far-fetched as it seems. In fact, some indoor pools share their pedigree with gyms. One of these places, called—what else?—Swim-Gym, belongs to Beverly Hills High School. While the pool itself was built during the New Deal era, the gym floor wasn't added until 1939. The facility had a cameo appearance in the 1946 movie *It's a Wonderful Life*, among other Hollywood productions, and a simple internet search for the movie's pool party scene produces results that illustrate how the floor retracts with the help of motors that roll each half of the basketball court underneath the gym's bleachers.

Watching the scene on my computer screen I kept thinking about how humid and smelling of chlorine the place must've been for all those actors and actresses dressed in their suits and dresses. Also, how many times has the floor been replaced? The current state-of-the-art floor, which was put on in 2016, allegedly due to extensive water damage, sits about 5 feet above the 25-yard pool and uses materials and design meant to prevent moisture buildup. Nevertheless, I imagine the gym to be equipped with a powerful ventilation system, since water evaporation will not stop just because a fancy floor has been installed above the pool. Those of us who've ever lived in a place with high precipitation rates know that wood and water do not mix and staining the former to protect it against the latter is a perennial chore.

This may also be why some pools are built with materials that require minimum maintenance. For instance, the Westwood Recreational Center and the Venice High School pool, both in Los Angeles, have pool decks made of concrete.

What's more, the locker rooms also have concrete floors. Unlike the indoor pools, decks, and locker rooms in Europe, which are often laid out in tile, American pools not only have a cheaper appearance, but are also, frankly, unpleasant to walk barefoot on. With the concrete feeling rough on the feet, one has the sensation of walking on a city sidewalk. But they must be easier to clean, no doubt—all you need is a hose and a wire broom.

The utility of such pools, however, is unquestionable, as is the low cost of construction, which is further helped by the temperate climate. With admission tickets costing a few dollars per visit, I am surprised that more people do not take advantage of it. Is this a matter of public awareness about water safety, which isn't an issue just in California but across the country? In her *New York Times* op-ed piece, Mara Gay, who sits on the paper's editorial board and is herself an avid ocean swimmer, calls attention to the fact that many people in the New York City don't know how to swim. "The city's free swim lessons program serves roughly 30,000 people every year at an annual cost of $2.5 million," she points out, citing city officials, before going on to underscore the shockingly small number of participants in a metro area that is home to some eight million residents. Part of the problem no doubt stems from the lack of adequate facilities, where people, especially children and adolescents, could take swim lessons. As Gay notes, "There are 50 operational public pools for more than eight million residents. Another 50 pools belong to the city's Department of Education, but only 27 of them are operational."[2] Is building more pools the answer to increasing water safety and awareness? Or is it more about making sure that existing pools are well-maintained? It's probably a little bit of both.

That I saw so many lanes underutilized during my visit to the Westwood pool is even more surprising because there are no time limits as to how long one can spend in the facility, unlike (again) in Europe, where pool operators often charge hourly rates and require that one pays extra for any time spent in the facility beyond the allotted time. If you subtract from the full hour the time it takes to get undressed and dressed—not to mention to take a shower after swimming—then the time one has for a swim dwindles down to about forty-five or fifty minutes. No wonder some customers find the system pricey. We have come a long way indeed from the Roman times, where public baths, known as thermae, not only helped the citizens maintain a proper hygiene and acted as social gatherings, but also stimulated the senses with their intricate design and atmospherics.

Still, keeping building costs down—especially in places where land is expensive—makes sense, especially if the costs associated with maintenance and operations can also be kept low. What's more, this strategy might also help bring swimming pools to communities that could not otherwise afford something beyond the basics offered by the nevertheless fast and fun-to-swim pool at Westwood.

This last point seems to apply to major swimming events as well. Over the last decade and a half, increasingly more swimming competitions have been held in temporary pools. Olympics, World Championships, US Olympic Swimming Trials—you name it, more and more organizers are tapping companies such as the Italy-based Myrtha Pools to erect and maintain the two pools—one for racing, the other for warming-up and cooling-down after the races—required for swim competitions. Given that a 50 meter, ten lane pool holds nearly a million gallons of water, it's a job that requires a great deal of expertise. The main reason why an organizer would elect to construct a temporary pool instead of relying on an existing facility has to do with wanting to attract the largest spectator crowd. American natatoriums—in Indianapolis or Federal Way, say—are excellent, but their bleacher space is limited; a temporary outdoor pool, with temporary bleachers on all four sides, can hold thousands more spectators. Additionally, these temporary pools are attractive because they can be erected seemingly anywhere. Who wouldn't want to watch the world's fastest swimmers in a basketball arena or at the beach?

If you are that swimmer who doesn't take pride in their chlorine-bleached hair or can't stand having a runny nose all the time due to the chemicals that help keep the water clean, then there is the option of swimming in lakes or ponds, not so much to take advantage of the freedom that open-water swimming provides, but rather to still do laps. Indeed, many swimmers love the idea of swimming in a lake where a section of it has been cordoned off with lane lines. This is the kind of a set-up that was available to Franz Kafka, who took lessons and went swimming in the Vltava River. According to Kafka's most recent biographer, Reiner Stach, there were several swimming schools along the banks of the river in Prague and most looked about the same:

> An expansive, floating wooden structure, which, in order to avoid destruction by drift ice, was retimbered every spring and then attached to the river bank with chains; inside there was a pool-like recess, known as the "mirror," with the river water flowing through; along the edges of the platform there were changing rooms, separate bathrooms, diving boards, and gymnastics equipment, as well as a small kitchen with a few restaurant tables at which coffee and beer were served.[3]

That Kafka remained a lifelong swimmer is kind of surprising, given the surviving photographs of him, in which he appears rather unathletic. What's more, Kafka was known to be painfully self-conscious about his body, which he found lacking in vigor, especially when compared to the swimming and beer-drinking crowd he would encounter at the riverside beach in summertime. Luckily, taking lessons, including from his father, who seemed bent on teaching his son proper technique—which Kafka addressed in his "Letter to His Father"—did not turn Kafka from swimming or any other aquatic activities, like kayaking and rowing. Stach observes that Kafka not only renewed his membership to a particular swimming school for years, even after he contracted tuberculosis, but while traveling on business sought places to swim immediately upon arrival. "The forces that drew him to the water," Stach writes, "must have been quite powerful, forces that enabled him to forget his fears, inhibitions, and social prickliness."[4] In other words, like many of us, the author of "Metamorphosis" felt happiest not on land but in water.

2 WHAT IS YOUR POOL?

As someone else put it, the story of swimming has no beginning or end. Ever since humans looked across water and either saw or wondered about the existence of the other shore, they have tried to reach it—by boat, by attaching makeshift wings to their shoulders, and by swimming—and a swimming pool puts that goal within our reach. In the swimming pool—outdoor, indoor—we can both forget who we are and dream of becoming someone else, which is why we swim for pleasure, exercise, and relaxation. However, swimming pools are a nuisance to some homeowners grandfathered into owning and maintaining them; that's a separate tale, one that no swimming fanatic like myself wants to hear. Or am I wrong? After all, countless people meet their end in swimming pools, and not every pool is a swimming pool. Olympic-caliber natatoriums and the kidney-shaped backyard sensations that dot Southern California's landscape may have the same pedigree, but they serve different purposes and are perceived differently by their owners and patrons.

The common denominator of the attraction that swimming pools hold for us is the belief that the structure can help transform us. The second we get in the water, we enter a realm that's both exciting and dangerous, but who of us hasn't felt that only in the pool can we forget our worries and come clean of the grime of a hard day. Pushing off the wall and taking that first stroke or just floating on our backs, we literally let go of things and focus on being one with the water. Ten, fifteen, twenty strokes later we reach the other end of a 25-yard pool, look around, and get ready to do it all over again. Along the way we stare at the black line painted on the bottom, which guides us, letting us know whether we're swimming in the middle of the lane and how far we are from the wall. In the meantime, the water caresses us and, because it resists any body disturbing its placid surface, makes us feel physically strong.

This combination of pleasure and effort captivates the hearts and imaginations of countless of people, including artists who have turned pools into representations of our fears and desires. No wonder the casinos in Las Vegas have invested in pool designs with elements of grandiose architectural styles and various time periods. Every swimming pool acts as a reproduction of an open body of water, representing new beginnings—for many immigrants literally so; a casino pool is both a place to hide and a place to partake in an ancient ritual of rebirth or baptism.

In William Henry Jackson's photograph, *Bathing Pool at the Casino, Palm Beach, Florida* (ca. 1880-97), for example, we are witness to a scene that wouldn't be out of place in Sin City.[1] The indoor pool is housed in a structure that's half-palace, half-opera house, what with multiple columns and archways on three sides of the pool and a set of curved concrete stairs disappearing into the water at the far end.

The nine men in the murky water must've been told to hold still by the photographer, as have some of the casino guests looking on from the floor above. In fact, while the swimmers are dressed in knee-long body suits, the standard swimming attire at the time and for several decades afterward, something about them gives them the look of circus performers. It could be that one of the men is standing on the shoulders of another, posing, with his fists against his hips. Or that there are ropes with triangular handles hanging from the ceiling. Indeed, the location of the pool itself makes it look like a courtyard, where—if this were a land-based scene—entrainers of various kinds showcase their tricks and skills. One of the other swimmers, it must be said, is looking through what looks like a lifesaving ring. While the depth of water isn't too great, for most of the men are standing, it is a good thing a lifesaving device is part of the scene, if only because the casino patrons, dressed in their Sunday-best, don't appear ready or willing to jump in should a swimmer needed to be rescued.

If the casino pool discussed above also reminds us of a bathhouse, albeit a large bathhouse, that's not surprising. After all, before there were pools, there were bathhouses. The men in the photograph may or may not have been swimming, but their poses suggest they were likely there to play or simply enjoy being submerged in water. Which is why I find it important to point out that there is a difference between a pool and a swimming pool.

Al Fenn's 1950 photograph of a GM dump truck whose bed has been filled with 7000 gallons of water is a case in point. Part of the 1955 General Motors Powerama, the Euclid model, GM's largest truck in production at the time, was exhibited among other technological and engineering marvels, including small solar-powered cars. Designing a truck that can carry the weight of thousands of gallons of water is no small feat, and I assume the point was also to suggest that the Euclid could be equipped with all sorts of beds, including a watertight one, but the main credit still goes to the company's marketing staff. While the photograph includes a decent crowd of curious onlookers, the 'pool on wheels' itself looks tiny and not suitable for swimming.

Indeed, the two women in the photo appear to be all about sunbathing and cooling off in the water—that is what can be inferred from looking at the props placed in and (mostly) around the pool. With the roof of the cab turned into a deck, there is just enough space for two, perhaps three people to lay out on their towels. What's best about the set-up is that it contains a diving board. Secured to the cab's roof, right between the two sunbathing spots, the board extends not only over the pool, as it should, but forward, over the truck's engine, which suggests that one might be able to perform a short run-up before bouncing off the board and diving or jumping into the water. This pool also comes with a lifesaving ring—marked "S.S. Euclid"—and a ladder for climbing in and out.

An internet search produces more photographs of this curio, and in one of them we see a third person, a man wearing a captain's hat and diving into the pool. I must admit that upon first seeing the diving board I took it to be a fake, one of those things that comes with the scene but is rather impractical and thus just for show. My skepticism about its utility stemmed from questioning the depth of the truck's bed—is it deep enough for diving and not just any diving but diving off a diving board? I wondered. The bounce one can get even on a small board would seem to render this set-up not just unusable but dangerous. Perhaps that's why the left edge of the truck's bed is rimmed with a railing— or is that just another contraption intended to make the truck look like a ship? Well, the diver is clearly going for it. Immortalized mid-air, with his arms spread out, he is about to make a splash. Is he going to break his form and instead of piking straighten up and go in feet first? The fact that I'm even asking myself this question makes this a great picture. If pressed, I would say he's going to jump rather than dive into the water, given how in this bird's eye view picture he is about to overshoot the bed and land on the pavement beside the truck.

In the meantime, the water spilled on the ground tells us the actors or models have been having plenty of fun. But how did the truck come to be filled with all that water? Was it first driven to its spot, then filled with water from a cistern? I doubt any of the spectators, even if they included trucking or construction or mining company executives, would buy the Euclid for its ability to do anything other than to haul tons of dirt or rocks, etc. But who knows. Quarries and mines connote back-breaking work (not to mention environmental degradation), and they are sites we most often associate with the type of a giant-wheel truck like the Euclid. Providing a little R&R in the form of a pool on wheels sounds great, if a little ridiculous, too, but again we can thank the marketing folks for that.

A pool on wheels or a pool in the ground—it doesn't matter. The idea is the same: fun in the sun. Real estate developers operating in temperate climates have long marketed the idea of a backyard pool as site of luxury, something to be desired and envied. Indeed, as the historian Lawrence Culver has observed,

> The movement of family social life and leisure time into the backyard, and the construction of patios, barbecues, and swimming pools, allowed suburbanites to live a resort lifestyle year-round, at least as long as weather permitted. . . . In 1949 there were 10,000 private swimming pools in the United States. In 1959 there would be more than 250,000; 90,000 were located in Los Angeles.[2]

Pools came in different sizes, from the seemingly ubiquitous kidney-shaped curio, to the simple, some might say boring, rectangular hole in the ground. The size and shape of a backyard pool—and whether it came with an adjacent jacuzzi or not—was often dictated by space and budget constraints, which is still the case today, but in terms of style and design, the so-called infinity pool eventually became the choice for many pool enthusiasts.

Unlike most pool designs, the infinity pool gives pool-goers a sense of being unconstrained, which does not work for lap-swimming, but lends itself to leisurely swimming, where the swimmer's head does not get submerged and the concept of side-breathing does not apply. Doing the breaststroke, for instance, while keeping one's head above the water, or some form of doggy paddling, could make the pool feel endless indeed. This sensation would be heightened by an overflow gutter. A body moving through water produces a wake, which bounces off the pool's walls, producing turbulence. An overflow gather fixes this problem by letting the water flow over the edge of the pool and into the gutter. Not all infinity pools have overflow gutters; some are constructed so that the water simply spills out of the pool and onto the deck. Given that many outdoor-pool meccas are in regions affected by draught, some form of water reclamation applies, but in ways that do not diminish the idea of an infinity pool as an outdoor body of water, blending in seamlessly with the backyard or the surrounding landscape.

The overflow gutter has also come to revolutionize the sport of competitive swimming. By diminishing the amount of water sloshing around in the pool, the design lowers the amount of turbulence produced by a swimmer. Now imagine eight or ten swimmers racing in the same pool at the same time; without the overflow gutter, the athletes would have to contend not only with their own wake but also that of their competitors. Back in the day before the overflow gutter on the long sides of a pool, the outside lanes, lanes 1 and 8, were considered the slowest, even if the pool had built-in gutters inside the walls, which, if they were wide enough, did a pretty good job of allowing the wake to escape. Improvements in lane line design and manufacturing have likewise played a role in diminishing swimmer-produced turbulence, not unlike a breakwater erected to protect a coast or an entrance into a harbor.

However, the lane lines also took away the sensation of openness associated with infinity pools. In fact, it seems that the infinity pool came with a contradiction built into its design. An infinity pool positioned on a cliff overlooking the ocean is a beautiful sight, a small body of water mirroring, as it were, that of its boundless antecedent, but due to the water line in infinity pools being somewhat unclear, it is tricky to perform flip turns in them, for the risk of painfully striking the edge of the pool with one's heels. A pool with lane lines designating each lane, on the other hand, makes no secret about its purpose and utility as a place for lap-swimming.

Arguably most lap swimmers dislike swimming in pools with no lane lines demarcating their space and direction of swimming. Turbulence is bad, yes, but not as bad as having someone else swim into you. When sharing a lane, swimmers mimic the direction of the flow of traffic on a road, that is, by "hugging the lane line" to the right of them. Sometimes, at international competitions, when the pool is open for warm-up before the main competition begins, swimmers from countries that drive on the left and those that drive on the right side of the road end up bumping into each other. It's a harmless reminder that the world is a varied place, even when it comes to swimmers and pool rules.

Lane lines, which used to be nothing more than ropes strung with pieces of cork or Styrofoam, make a pool look symmetrical, too. Moreover, while it's not quite the same as a chessboard or a tennis court, since swimmers do not perform lateral or diagonal moves, a pool equipped with lane lines suggests movement. Both qualities are on display in Galit Seligmann's photograph of the North Sydney Olympic Pool, which opened in 1936 and played host to the 1938 British Empire Games.[3] Australia being a well-known and enthusiastic supporter of all kinds of physical activity, including, improbably, winter sports, it's perhaps no surprise that swimmers and pool-goers of all abilities share the pool in the shadow of the Sydney Harbour Bridge, where nearly a hundred swimming world-records were set between 1953 and 1978.

Indeed, in the photograph by Seligmann, the eight-lane facility appears to accommodate patrons of all level and abilities. The lane closest to the viewer, lane 8, has only four people in it. They are facing away from the wall; they seem to be looking across the other lanes at what's going on in lane 1, the lane closest to the waters of the Sydney Harbour, which is visible through a glass fence incorporated into Art Deco arches that resemble doorways or high windows. What's more, the swimmers appear to be floating or treading the water, and only one of them has a cap and goggles on. Are they in the pool for a session of aquarobics, which has become ubiquitous at pools all over the world? I don't see any speakers blaring old hits, so perhaps they are simply there to cool off. Which isn't the case with the folks in the remaining lanes. The far lane, lane 1, seems to be occupied by an organized group—a youth swim team? It would appear so, given the size of the swimmers doing the backstroke in that lane as well as the fact that when we look diagonally across the pool, we see a group of swimmers congregating at the wall and awaiting instructions from their coach. A lane line that would normally be hung between lanes 1 and 2 has been taken out and in its place two ropes have been put it, de facto turning the far lane into two narrow lanes needed to accommodate the large practice group.

The pool's remaining lanes are designated as lap lanes, with each assigned to a particular swimming speed. Of the five lanes, the middle ones are for the fastest swimmers, thus reflecting the lane assignments in competitive swimming, where lane 4 goes to the fastest qualifier from the morning heats, lane 5 to the second fastest, lane 3 to the third fastest, and so on. The swimmers are mimicking the rules of driving in Australia by swimming on the left side of the lane, and their movement is further accentuated by the lines, curves and arches of the Sydney Harbour Bridge, which sits at an angle above them, with the shells of the Sydney Opera House visible beyond the sun deck.

The steel bridge is a major thoroughfare for car, train, bike, and pedestrian traffic, and it's easy to imagine the amount of noise emanating from it. How do the pool patrons feel about it? I would imagine that some not only don't mind it, but appreciate it, for it might remind them that the world does not stand at a standstill and so they shouldn't either. On the other hand, it is equally plausible that many of the swimmers appreciate being able to tune out the noise of a major city going about its business just steps away from them. Submerged in water, they conquer each length of the pool listening to their bodies: a mixed tape of heartbeat and the exhilarating feeling that comes with being able to move effortlessly through water.

* * *

Skinny-dipping in a lake is a rite of passage for many people. It's hard to say whether its allure stems more from the desire to feel free or from the risk of being seen but not caught. While not all homeowners with pools enjoy the kind of privacy they wish they had, it goes without saying that most have at some point enjoyed their backyard jewel in the buff. Just ask the Huntington Beach-born and based documentary photographer Deanna Templeton, whose photographs of naked people swimming (in both black and white and color) have been collected in her volume *The Swimming Pool*.[4]

Writing in his Afterword to the book, the photographer's husband, Ed Templeton, states,

> [T]he nude swimmer is floating in a void of quiet solitude, the gentle pressure of being underwater enclosing her form like a baby in a womb and nothing exists outside of this world. A lone figure amidst a sea of blues and greys and frenetic sunlight performing a solitary dance for the photographer above, choosing movements and directions, twisting and swooping, contorting and expelling breaths painting a picture of form and light together.[5]

While each photograph provides only a still frame of the actions described in the afterword, the sense of movement is very much on display. This is particularly true in *Erin* (2015), where the assumed eponymous female is photographed underwater, with a string of air bubbles of various sizes floating to the surface behind her. The silhouette of her form is reflected underneath her, on the bottom of the pool, which she is practically skirting. But she is not looking at herself; with her back slightly arched and her head titled backward, she seems to be resurfacing after a quick dive. Like most of Deanna Templeton's subjects, she is young and in good shape, unencumbered by the photographer's lens or the constraints of the underwater world itself.

The series was born after an impromptu shoot of Ed Templeton swimming naked in a pool, and the volume collects photographs taken over a period of eight years. What's no less fascinating is the collection's title. Why "swimming pool" and not "naked swimmers"? After all, the photographs are more about depicting the human body, its shapes and form, rather than the vessel of water in which they happen to perform various movements. Like all the models—friends and acquaintances of Deanna Templeton—the red-haired woman immortalized in *Erin* could be mistaken for a water-borne creature, perhaps a fantastical mermaid—that's how in her element she appears. The perfect combination of just the right amount of bright light, her slightly tanned body, and the bluish tinge of the pool imbue the scene with a sense of dreamy litheness. The weight of the world—or just her days—is no longer on her shoulders. Paradoxically, it is the air bubbles that bring her and us, the viewers, back to reality. They signal that the underwater pleasure cruise must come to an end because, one might add tautologically, our bodies were not meant to live suspended and at ease in the liquid world.

Nevertheless, the human form has always been a thing to marvel at. A few decades before Templeton, it was David Hockney's paintings and photographs, especially those taken with a Polaroid camera, that aimed to depict the carefree and hedonistic bodies in water or by the poolside. The March 1982 photographs—featuring Nathan, Brian, and Gregory— are striking examples of Hockney's wish to depict the human form by way of fragmenting it. In that sense, the montage of a series of photographs goes a long way in suggesting an unstable environment, not unlike the physical, political, and social landscape of Southern California, and not just in the early stage of Reagan's White House, but in general.

"I came to Los Angeles for two reasons," says David Hockney, "The first was a photo by Julius Shulman of Case Study House #21, and the other was AMG's Physique Pictorial."[6] The Stahl House photographed by Julius Shulman and located in Hollywood Hills continues to be visited by locals and tourists alike, while *Physique Pictorial*, the legendary 'beefcake' magazine, folded decades ago. However, the clear lines of the modernist architectural masterpiece and the Classically inspired celebrations of the muscled body featured in the quarterly are seen in many a work by Hockney, including *A Bigger Splash* from 1967.

Created with acrylic paint while Hockney was teaching at UC Berkeley, the painting painstakingly reproduces an image captured initially with a camera. In the words of one critic and curator at Tate Britain, "the picture's title and the ejaculatory form of the splash, laboriously painted with a small brush over several weeks, perverts the abstract expressionists' concept of action painting and finding images 'in the moment.'"[7] *A Bigger Splash* isn't the only Hockney painting in which he uses a diving board as a conduit for the viewers to enter the picture, but it may be the sole painting in which the surface of the pool presented therein isn't placid. Furthermore, while the most conspicuous absence in the picture is that of the diver disappearing into the pool, there are also no identifying details that would pertain to the setting. Sure, the tall palm trees to the left of the modern house as well as those reflected in the sliding doors leading out and onto the deck of the pool are often used as stand-ins for Los Angeles, but the absence of any participants in the scene, let alone someone whom we might call a homeowner is eerie in and of itself.

Instead of people, we get a commentary on how lonely life can feel in a place like Los Angeles despite the beautiful sunlight and the nearly constant clear skies. The diving board, painted at an angle to the pool, which seems odd, given that diving boards typically lead straight out over the water, appears to be pointed directly at the lone folding chair set out on the deck. But the chair is empty, which further makes one wonder if the diver making the eponymous splash went into the pool not from the diving board but rather, after getting up from the chair, by simply jumping in from the side of the pool.

In any case, there is a performative aspect embedded in the painting's narrative: whoever it is that has gone into the pool—was it by way of a cannonball or a beautifully executed somersault?—has no audience except, of course, us. And we, in turn, are forced to take in the spectacle that's been captured here, thanks to the framing device around the image, which makes the latter feel cropped, even taken out of context. Is the so-called captive audience what is required to stand out in a hype-and-dreamer-saturated landscape of Los Angeles? The previous year, 1966, Hockney painted two smaller splash paintings, but this one stands out, not just for its size or bright color scheme, but also for freezing the moment when the pool's previously placid surface is disturbed enough to become something worthy of our attention. In a way, the painting isn't about the splash; in fact, the splash, however sexual its connotations, is the rupture at the heart of the before and the after of the narrative hinted at in the painting.

The freeze-framing of a moment is also at work in one of David Hockney's most famous paintings, the 1972 acrylic on canvas *Portrait of an Artist (Pool with Two Figures)*. That the image was chosen to grace the cover of the catalogue for the major retrospective of the artist's work that opened at Tate Britain in February 2017 isn't arbitrary. The painting belongs to the period when Hockney created double-portraits, that is, paintings that were based on photographs of his friends and acquaintances. The scene depicted in *Portrait of an Artist* was apparently "suggested by the accidental juxtaposition of two photographs, one, taken in Hollywood in 1966, of a boy swimming under water, the other of another boy gazing at the ground. Seeing them placed together, Hockney realized that he had a subject for a two-figure composition with a greater than usual dramatic charge."[8] The charge was further dramatized by Hockney's decision to depict in the painting Peter Schlesinger soon after the end of their relationship.

What is most fascinating about this painting, then, is the connection between the two men. Is the fully clothed man standing at the edge of the pool and looking down on the water seeing a reflection of himself, or is he there to greet the man swimming? After all, the man wearing a white speedo and doing the breaststroke under water could be just another swimmer exercising in a beautiful setting. Given that the work was created in the aftermath of a relationship that ended abruptly, it is plausible that Hockney thought of the swimmer as another man entering Peter's life, which is why the man under water is depicted abstractly. But Peter doesn't appear too excited about the man; in fact, his facial expression is rather tense, and the three layers of clothes he has on do not suggest that he is about to take a plunge and join the man in the pool.

The swimming pool itself makes me think this painting is more about self-reflection than anything else. With half of it painted as clear and the other half as murky, the painting seems to suggest a division that renders one's own feelings and emotions as inaccessible. Both halves also imply instability, the way that water isn't stable or placid in a pool with someone swimming it. The clear section's bottom resembles a mosaic—ripples or a map of many small countries with uneven borders—and the painting hints at the fact that each one of us is a composite of experiences and thoughts that rarely if ever coalesce into a neat narrative. Finally, that the pool scene—again, full of contrasting patterns—is set against the backdrop of a perfectly rendered idyllic landscape further denotes a level of turmoil in the mind of the young man standing on deck.

With a little encouragement from his imagination, he might still end up confronting head-on his own self in the cool, if turbulent, water of the swimming pool. And even if he fails to make sense of his circumstances—let alone figure out who he truly is—he will at least be able to untether himself from the world around him. Freed from gravity's pull, he will float on his back and bounce off the walls. He will spit the water out of his mouth like some Roman statue. In that sense he will both contribute to the ongoing idealization of private swimming pools and underscore the mirage-like nature of the entire enterprise, especially if we consider the consequences of climate change, which grow more dire with each season, each year.

3 WHY DO YOU SWIM?

When I queried friends and colleagues about examples of depictions of pools and swimming in film and literature, most responded with a quizzical look and made a sound that fell somewhere between a tsk and a tongue-click, then blurted out *The Great Gatsby* by F. Scott Fitzgerald and, especially, "The Swimmer" by John Cheever. *Of course*, I would respond, making a note to myself to re-read the famous short story set in New York State's Westchester County.

The story's opening sentence suggests that we are in for a humdrum of suburban bric-a-brac, what with the narrative being set on a midsummer Sunday afternoon and the main characters confessing to overindulging in alcohol the night before. Did they—Donald and Helen Westerhazy and their guests, Neddy and Lucinda Merrill—carouse together, or could it be that the Westerhazys's pool, with its green water sourced from an artesian well, just happens to be the place for the friends to congregate at the day after their escapades? Neddy—who's also referred to as Ned—Merrill might be the father of four daughters, but he hasn't lost any of his vigor or vitality.

When we meet him at the start of the story, which is set against the backdrop of perfect weather (despite the massive cumulous cloud seen in the distance), we learn that "He had been swimming and now he was breathing deeply, stertorously, as if he could gulp into his lungs the components of that moment, the heat of the sun, the intenseness of his pleasure."[1] That the splash in the pool got his metabolism going and made him feel less hungover and thus better goes without saying, but so did the glass of gin he was already nursing. In fact, he must have felt pretty good if he decided to cover the eight miles that separated the backyard pool oasis from his and Lucinda's waterside home.

One can imagine scenes like this being repeated all over the country, but I'd guess most to result in something no less extravagant but decidedly more private, like climbing onto the roof of the house and diving into the pool. In Neddy's case, he was an explorer—a new Magellan or Vasco de Gama—seemingly able "to see, with a cartographer's eye, that string of swimming pools, that quasi-subterranean stream that curved across the county."[2] Completely in his element while swimming down what he quickly dubbed the Lucinda River, he would pay a visit to fourteen households and their pools along his journey, expecting to be greeted, unlike those Portuguese adventurers, by adoring crowds. This was so at the first stop, the Grahams, where Mrs. Graham, who it turns out had been trying to get a hold of Neddy all morning, offers him a drink. Perhaps surprising even himself, Neddy quickly realized that "the hospitable customs and traditions of the natives would have to be handled with diplomacy if he was ever going to reach his destination."[3] Otherwise, he might end up like one of those runners participating in a beer run, which includes drinking a lager or an IPA every mile or so, and that would not be kosher.

So, on he goes, or rather, swims, toward his house in Bullet Park. At some of the houses he encounters no one, this being a midsummer Sunday, while at the Bunkers's place "Prosperous men and women gathered by the sapphire-colored waters while caterer's men in white coats passed them cold gin."[4] Upon seeing him, Mrs. Bunker reacts as if he were her most prized guest and savior. Unable to get away, Neddy is led to the bar through an adoring throng of women who want to kiss him and men who want to shake his hand. A gin and tonic is placed in his hand, but then he knows better and, like a superhero, manages to slip away just in time, buoyed by his sense of mission. It is only at the next house, which belongs to the Levys who seemed to have just left their house—for another party? Church service?—that Neddy is content to take a break. He has swum half of the Lucinda River by now. His fourth and fifth drinks, which he pours himself, feel earned.

By then, however, the cumulous cloud seen earlier hovering in the distance seems to have grown more ominous. There is thunder. Indeed, the soundscape of Ned's surroundings intensifies, and he becomes acutely aware of a train whistle and birdsongs changing ahead of the storm. There is a sound of water rushing out of fountains.

"Then there was an explosion, a smell of cordite, and rain lashed the Japanese lanterns that Mrs. Levy had bought in Kyoto the year before last, or was it the year before that?"[5] Seemingly unsure of the direction he should take next—at a public facility he would be kept away from the pool for thirty minutes due to lightning—even though we are told that Ned has always liked stormy weather, he elects to wait out the storm in the Levy's gazebo. Time stops for Ned, or at least loses its meaning. He doesn't abandon his pursuit, with the goal of swimming home still very much on his mind, but by now the things of this world, things that Ned might have previously ignored, come into sharp focus. He is cold for the first time, too.

When he encounters a pool drained of water at the Welchers's, he wonders about when he spoke to them last. An empty pool was just not something one saw in Westchester County. Mystified and apprehensive, he walks to the front of the house and sees a for-sale sign, which makes him wonder if his memory is failing or if he's found a way to repress unpleasant facts. It's the sound of a game of tennis being played nearby that evens him out and sets up the final leg of his journey.

But now he's no longer a man at the top of his game. Crossing roads and highways he was "laughed at, jeered at, a beer can was thrown at him, and he had no dignity or humor to bring to the situation."[6] Cheever, like the master storyteller that he was, brings his hero down to size and thus creates a conflict that's playing out both internally and externally.

But was the doubt that begins to creep into Ned's mind only a clever formal trick to introduce another interlude to the story, or a genuine development? By this point, the story has shifted to the second person, and we're brought into the story as more than adoring fans or onlookers—we become arbiters of Ned's existential crisis brought on by his athleticism, vanity, and the fact of having had too much to drink not just the night before but in general. "At what point had this prank, this joke, this piece of horseplay become serious?" Ned asks himself, but we suspect that it never was just a joke.[7] He contemplates turning back, but then pushes on.

The next stop along the Lucinda River is a public pool, with its posted rules and regulations, surely something that Neddy wasn't used to seeing, let alone adhering to. But he does as the sign says, and he takes a shower and washes his feet before entering the pool. He finds the smell of chlorine suffocating and the obdurate lifeguards police-like. Every journey includes its own share of unpleasant encounters and disappointments, alas, though the fact that Ned dislikes sharing the water with others is telling of his social standing and expectations of how others ought to behave around him. When the lifeguards blow their whistles at him—because he's not wearing some kind of ID badge—he gets out of there as quickly as possible.

The Hallorans—Ned's next stop—were a retired couple suspected of harboring Communist sympathies, but neither that nor their preference for swimming and lounging around their pool nude bothered Ned. In fact, before entering the premises, he drops his trunks. The couple seems indifferent upon seeing him, and after a quick explanation as to what he's doing, the conversation switched—thanks to Mrs. Halloran—to talking about how sorry they felt to hear about his misfortunes, which included having to sell the house. Ned doesn't understand what she means, but he also does not press the subject; instead, as he's leaving, he takes stock of his body, and wonders about having lost weight during his journey. "His arms were lame. His legs felt rubbery and ached at the joints. The worst of it was the cold in his bones and the feeling that he might never be warm again."[8] In fact, everything around him seems out of whack, too. Early on he meditated on the sight of a maple tree stripped by the storm of its leaves, but now there were even more leaves spinning through in the air around him and he could smell wood smoke—in the middle of summer! He needs a drink to pick him up, but when he arrives at the Eric and Helen Saches's pool, he is disappointed to learn that the house has been dry since Eric's operation three years ago. How could he have forgotten about that? Ned wonders and goes on to chastise himself once again about the state of his memory. Was he really a failed husband and father?

He hasn't been a good neighbor, at least not to the Biswangers, who were having a great party. Once spotted by the host, Grace Biswanger, he is immediately marked as a party crasher, and reprimanded for not accepting any of the many dinner invitations that the Biswangers sent him and Lucinda over the years. He did not belong there in another sense of the word as well, for he found the Biswangers too good at networking, the kind of people who invited half the town to their parities and talked shamelessly about money. They were schmoozers, in other words, but Mrs. Biswanger also alludes, to some of her guests, to troubles that seemed to have befallen the Merrills.

The early evening turns to night. Neddy's last three stops—at the residence of his former mistress, the exchange with whom did not, as he had expected, lift his spirits; at the Gilmartins's, where "for the first time in his life, he did not dive" into the pool but rather used the steps to enter the water; and finally at the Clydes's—made him realize how defeated he felt despite having completed his goal of swimming across the county.[9] Depleted physically and mentally, he arrived at his house, but the doors were locked, the lights out. "He tried the garage doors to see what cars were in, but the doors were locked, and rust came off the handles onto his hands."[10] He used whatever strength he had left to shout and pound his fists against the door, then, when he peered through the windows, he saw that the house was empty.

What happened to Lucinda and their four daughters? Was the journey just a figment of his imagination? Did he drink so much and often that the metaphor of water as a source of birth and rebirth turned sinister? The story alludes to water as a conduit that amplifies sounds, including voices, but perhaps we'll never know for sure if the swims and conversations took place only in Ned's drunken stupor. Stripped in the end of everything by the water he traversed time and again, the main character is left with nothing, a mere scaffolding of his dreams and aspirations.

* * *

This is quite different, at least initially, from the premise of Billy Wilder's *Sunset Boulevard*. The 1950 film features William Holden as Joe Gillis, a struggling screenwriter who is being harassed by men trying to repossess his car. During one of the episodes when he's fleeing from them, he blows a tire and ends up turning off Sunset Blvd. into the driveway of a deserted-looking mansion. These days, most houses along Sunset do not look deserted at all and are cordoned off from the street by tall fences, brick walls, and/or tall hedges. What hasn't changed, however, is the figure of a struggling or underemployed screenwriter who toils in obscurity, hoping to sell their script, which, even if it were to happen, would most likely never be made into a film or TV show.

The film is just as famous for its swimming pool scene as it is for playing up the dreams of the masses who move to Los Angeles in hopes of making it in the movie industry. In fact, one might argue that the pool, like the proverbial glass that's either half empty or half full, is meant to reflect the aspiration of the film's main characters. Sure, when we first meet Joe, he is already dead and floating face down in the pool of the house located at 10086 Sunset Boulevard. But then, through flashback, we eventually learn how he met his end, and part of the journey includes seeing the pool drained of water, home to rats scurrying around the bottom.

That the house belongs to a forgotten movie star from the silent film era only adds another layer to the pool-as-metaphor. Norma Desmond (Gloria Swanson) lives in a fantasy world, with her huge house a storage space of bygone props and mementos. She craves attention and gets it only from Max, her butler who is himself a former director. The cocoon he's created for her, going as far as fabricating hundreds of fan letters that seem to arrive daily, is an echo chamber of vanity, and Joe's arrival only heightens the level of incomprehensibility that exists between Norma and the outside world. Like two people shouting to each other in a pool, where the water both carries their voices and muffles them, Norma and Joe eventually find a way to help each other out through real and pretend gestures.

It's hard to imagine, given the film's story line, that the pool got used much, but of course, as an object of desire, it was a must-have then as it is now. Unlike the Great Palaestra at the ruins of Pompeii—"a vast square 150 yards by 140, far larger than a modern football field, surrounded on three sides by a portico"[11]—which included at its center a pool with a sloping bottom, Norma's pool does not seem intended for lap-swimming. This is not unusual—even today most pool owners do not as much as dip or frolic in their pools. This is partly why the pool-design industry keeps evolving by incorporating lightshows and such into their design models. In fact, as Lynn Sherr writes in *Swim: Why We Love the Water*, "Today, almost no pool goes in without a water feature. They want to see the water move;

they want to hear it move, they want it to dance, to turn colors at night."[12] According to Howard Means, the author of *Splash! 10,000 Years of Swimming*, the palaestra at Pompeii did not come with any frills: "No frigidarium here. No laconicum either, and no changing rooms. This palaestra was purpose-driven—for sweating, for swimming, for competitions, and for the annual exhibitions put on by the *collegium iuvenum*, Pompeii's equivalent of a municipal sports organization."[13]

What about Norma's pool? Even before she and Joe come to terms about his doctoring of her unwieldy script, he is forced to stay at the mansion, in a guest house with a view of the empty pool with three ladders and a diving board. Like the main house, the pool has seen better days, but it also reminds Joe of the fact that he's always wanted a house with a pool. Alas, Joe never quite settles into his role. He pays lip service to Norma and her desire to once again be the world's biggest movie star while trying hard to hold on to his own dream of striking Hollywood gold.

Exhausted by Norma's demands, Joe packs up his things and leaves, ready to take that small-town paper job back in his home state of Ohio; he rushes back to the house upon hearing the news that Norma slit her wrists. He seems resigned to being Norma's lover. We see them lounging by the pool, in one scene; in another, he gets out of the water, trim and fit. In the meantime, a script screener for Paramount Pictures tries to reach him about some of his old projects. "No one leaves a star. That's what makes one a star," is one of

Norma's bon mots, a statement whose pretentiousness comes to sinister fruition at the end of the movie.

Indeed, at five in the morning a call comes in, reporting a murder. A big star is involved. When police and reporters show up, a body of a young man is discovered floating in the pool at Norma's Mediterranean mansion, the aftermath of the scene in which Joe attempts to leave Norma who's brandishing a pistol and once again threatening to kill herself. Joe has been shot three times, with two bullets in the back and one in the stomach. He is dressed in a suit and wearing a striped tie. When the police storm the house and try to interrogate Norma, she thinks it's all a movie set, and acts accordingly.

Film history books tell us that the pool scene was initially filmed with cameras positioned in the water, but, given the technology available then, it's hard to imagine that the shots would have been of adequate quality. A blurry picture might have suited a different context, one in which Joe Gillis's character had completely lost his bearings on reality, but that's not what transpires in the film.

Joe's eyes and mouth are also open, perhaps suggesting that's he's finally getting his fill of the lifestyle he always wanted. One might argue that the mirrors, which were placed on the bottom of the pool, give us a clear reflection of Holden's character, implying the film's creators wish for the audiences to see themselves in Joe, on the one hand, and be haunted by him, on the other. Norma Desmond may be a grotesque character, and it's easy to ridicule her, but *Sunset*

Boulevard is a classic of film noir. Acquiescing to her vision of triumphant return, Norma turns Joe Gills into a Faustian character, no matter his change of heart at the end, and the pool into a metaphor for status-seeking and the inscrutability of human wants and desires.

In this context, it is interesting, I think, to bring up, if briefly, the famous pool scene in Book Two of Vladimir Nabokov's novel, *Lolita* (1955). Believing that Lolita has left him, Humbert looks for her everywhere, then spots her near the motel pool, playing fetch with a dog. While he's calming down, the scene takes a turn for the worse. It's Lolita's youthful energy that sets off Hubert. "Suddenly," he tells us,

> something in the pattern of her motions, as she dashed this way and that in her Aztec Red bathing briefs and bra, struck me … there was an ecstasy, a madness about her frolics that was too much of a glad thing. Even the dog seemed puzzled by the extravagance of her reactions. I put a gentle hand to my chest as I surveyed the situation. The turquoise blue swimming pool some distance behind the lawn was no longer behind that lawn, but within my thorax, and my organs swam in it like excrements in the blue sea water in Nice.[14]

What provoked this kind of reaction? It couldn't have just been Lolita's delicate vigor. Sure enough, another man has entered the scene. "One of the bathers had left the pool and, half-concealed by the peacock shade of trees, stood quite still, holding the ends of the towel around his neck and following Lolita with his amber eyes."[15] Resembling, to Humbert, a satyr—the mythological part-man, part-goat figure sporting an erection—the man not only stirs in Humbert feelings of manly insecurity, but also simply angers him, especially since Lolita seems fully aware that someone is staring at her. But then the ogler takes on a human form, that of Humbert's Swiss cousin, Gustave Trapp, the "Detective Trapp" figure that Humbert believes is following him and Lolita as they venture farther out west. Is he a figment of Humbert's imagination? The whole thing unnerves him, and indicates how his jealousy and possessiveness have turned his mind into a receptacle of the fantastical and imaginary.

This kind of mental combat can manifest itself in physical anguish, of course, but the opposite is equally true, where being unmoored can be both beautiful and harrowing. When Walt Whitman writes, in "I Sing the Body Electric" from *Leaves of Grass*, about a naked swimmer rolling around in the "heave of the water," he celebrates the human form being married with the elements.[16] On the other hand, the contemporary poet Carl Phillips, in his poem, "Swimming," dives into water and then looks back and ponders the landscape, including its history. "But what hasn't been damaged?" he asks about the effects of storms and waves.[17] He is also internalizing this moment, finding himself to be an insignificant speck on the map of the universe. He swims, he floats, yes, but because the things—buildings, trees, lights—back on land go in and out of focus, he begins to feel untethered from it all. Being in the water allows him to lose himself in the vastness of the open water. The outcome translates into loneliness, but also a strange sense of belonging.

The late author and neurologist Oliver Sacks wrote many a book of his while swimming. As he put it in his brief essay, "Water Babies," "Theories and stories would construct themselves in my mind as I swam to and fro, or round and round Lake Jeff [Lake Jefferson]. Sentences and paragraphs would write themselves in my mind, and at such times I would have to come to shore every so often to discharge them."[18]

Unsurprisingly, Sacks loved the open water, but he also swam in a pool, at his local YMCA in Westchester, New York. He was even named Top Distance Swimmer there, he tells us, for swimming five hundred laps (he would've continued lest the officials hadn't stopped him). "Swimming" he writes, "gave me a sort of joy, a sense of well-being so extreme that it became at times a sort of extasy. There was a total engagement in the act of swimming, in each stroke, and at the same time the mind could float free, become spellbound, in a state like a trance."[19] Readers might appreciate knowing that Sacks's *A Leg to Stand On*, in which he writes about his own experience of patienthood, was written in the water: "My publisher was puzzled by the water smudges and the running ink on the manuscript, and insisted that I have it typed."[20]

* * *

For the Mardini sisters, Sara and Yusra, swimming was much more than an escape into their inner lives. No doubt years of training made them disciplined and resilient, able to handle setbacks in ways most of those who have not experienced a training regimen could not, but it wasn't until they made the decision to flee Syria for Germany that those skills became apparent.

The biopic film about the sisters called—what else?—*The Swimmers* (2022) opens with a scene featuring a pool in a suburb of Damascus.[21] Because the location stamp includes the year 2011, we are immediately aware of the incongruity of the pool scene with the brutal war that's been tearing up the country. Indeed, the pool scene is filled with carefree laughter and play. There are children learning how to swim and climbing onto blowup mattresses and crocodiles, adolescent boys jumping and diving into the pool, and a man or two crisscrossing the unchartered waters in an attempt to swim a few laps.

As the camera dips underwater, we are presented with a scene the opposite of that; we're still in the packed natatorium, but the underwater world is quiet, and not only because the sisters are challenging themselves to a breath-holding competition. The cheap pink wristwatch they use to time themselves seems out of place, but it also goes with the colorful and fun-loving crowd. Then the camera cuts to the two girls walking home, to a comfortable house where a surprise birthday party is being thrown for one of them. The framed pictures tell us that one of the girls, Yusra, is a star swimmer. Sara is a competitive swimmer, too, but it's clear that Yusra is the dad's favorite. The girls' dad is also their coach.

This proverbial quiet before the storm goes a long way to help dramatize what's coming, and the fact that we, the viewers, know what's coming doesn't make it any less heartbreaking. There are gunfights and bombs falling nearby. The events that had ushered in the so-called Arab Spring are playing out in Syria, too, but President Bashar al-Assad has no intentions of giving up power. Meanwhile, the Mardinis, like everyone else, are trying to carry on, as evidenced by the dad telling the party guests that he will be the first dad in history to have three daughters compete in the Olympics. We also witness a scene of the girls dancing to "Titanium" by David Guetta in a rooftop club while bombs are falling off in the distance. Syria, as the girls knew it, might no longer exist, but Yusra still dreams of going to the Olympics.

In the next scene we are at the pool, a 50-meter indoor pool with a propaganda billboard featuring the president overlooking it. The dad isn't happy with Yusra's swimming times. When they return home, they watch footage from the Beijing Olympics, studying Michael Phelps's technique during his gold-medal winning 100-meter butterfly race. The gleaming pool seen on the laptop screen is worlds from the reality on the ground in Damascus, but life somehow goes on—despite combat, power shortages, and sexual harassment, depicted poignantly in one scene. There is even time and place for a swimming competition.

In this pivotal scene, we see Yusra swimming the 100-meter butterfly race. She's leading the whole way and looks on track to not only win but also get a personal best time. Alas, before she can finish the second lap of the two-lap race, the pool comes under attack. The fans flee the stands, as bombs drop through the roof. One of them lands in the water, right in Yusra's lane. There is a moment of suspense, as we wait for the bomb to explode. Time has stopped. The bomb is slowly sinking to the bottom, but when it finally hits it, it doesn't explode. It's a dud. Afterward, the family agrees to let the sisters flee for Germany, joining the more than 5 million Syrian refugees who've fled their country because of the civil war.

Even though their father told them not to take the perilous sea route from Turkey to Greece, the girls do it anyway despite several ominous signs, especially the announcement they heard on the plane out of Syria, reminding the passengers that the life jackets belong to the airline and those caught stealing them will be prosecuted. When the cousin points out, somewhat lightheartedly, that they're refugees now, Yusra disagrees, saying they're not, because they have a home.

Before the three of them reach Germany, they experience everything we've been reading about in reports about the crossings, both through the Aegean Sea and via the land routes through Southeastern Europe. The part of the film in which the sisters cross the sea in a blowup pontoon—one that's only slightly larger and more suitable than the floaties we've seen in the opening scene—is stunning. Later, when they're safe, we learn that all Sara kept thinking of during that time was her parents and "How stupid it would be for swimmers to die in the sea." And indeed, the film suggests that the sisters survived the crossing because of their swimming background—they swam beside the dingy to lighten its load and thus keep it from sinking. The film plays up Yusra's single-minded focus on her Olympic goals by dropping imaginary lane lines into the sea. What are we supposed to make of it, in addition to admiring Yusra's ability to turn off the world and concentrate on the task at hand? Maybe that the water, while it kills countless refugees trying to reach Europe's shores, is also a conduit, a way forward.

Given the film's roots as an inspirational biopic, the girls make it to Germany and, thanks to Angela Merkel's generous refugee policy, are allowed to stay; it's worth pointing out that the first thing they see after the overnight journey from Budapest is Berlin's Memorial to the Murdered Jews of Europe. Is the film's director, Sally El-Hosaini, trying to connect the Holocaust with the plight of refugees, suggesting that the death of innocents continues, and that Europe will always commemorate some and forget others?

After languishing for months in a refugee camp at the Tempelhof Airport, Yusra starts working out—we see her performing various dryland exercises, such as lunges, pushups, etc.—and eventually, the sisters find a pool. They walk up to the coach, whose name is Sven, and Yusra tells him they want to join his team and train twice a day, because she hasn't given up on going to the Olympics. The coach doesn't know what to say, so he tells them there are no vacant spots on his team, but then—and this is the great thing about a quantifiable sport such as swimming—he learns of Yusra's best times, which are quite fast, and decides to give the girls a chance.

The rest of the film does a great job of illustrating the bureaucratic nightmare and existential limbo that refugees experience after some time in the so-called promised land. Many become disillusioned with their new surroundings and suffer various identity crises, even going as far as questioning their decision to leave their homelands. Sara and Yusra (and their cousin Nizir) are not immune to it, though in the case of the younger sister she manages to stay true to her dream of becoming a great swimmer, because, as she's put it, "Swimming is home for me." She comes closest to finding herself as a person and athlete in 50-meter pools—some of the training scenes are shot in an outdoor pool while others are filmed in an indoor facility, and the flume pool where Sven's *Wasserfreunde Spandau 04* team practices. After she and Sara have a heart-to-heart conversation about Yusra abandoning her dream of representing Syria and instead joining, after some nudging, the Refugees Olympic Team, we see Yusra sitting alone near the edge of the outdoor pool. It's nighttime. The pool is lit with underwater lights, which give it a sharp bluish tint. It's the proverbial blank canvas on which Yusra will write the rest of her story.

4 WHO GETS TO SWIM?

Writing in his introduction to *Backyard Oasis: The Swimming Pool in Southern California Photography, 1945-1982*, Daniell Cornell reminds us that while swimming pools have served a variety of functions throughout history, it was only in the first half of the twentieth century that their militaristic or athletic purpose began to give way to the purpose of leisure and relaxation. With time, however, swimming pools became contested by proponents and opponents of social and political changes sweeping the country (as did other American municipal public spaces, including parks and playgrounds). "Part of the appeal of suburban development," Cornell goes on to say, "was undoubtedly its immunity from these tensions facilitated by the suburb's physical segregation from urban heterogeneity."[1]

While one segment of the society advocated for desegregation, another constructed more and more private swimming pools that came to represent their ideals and material status, as evidenced by Ed Ruscha's 1968 *Nine*

Swimming Pools, which, like his other sequential works, both amuses and troubles. Because the photographs are cropped, the pools presented therein seem taken out of context, with hardly any of the adjacent houses or backyards included. In fact, the only thing that's common to all the pools, arguably, is the water, either still or rippled, ranging in hue from deep to light blue. One of the pools comes with lane markers painted on the bottom, suggesting it's a public pool, that is, a place where rules and regulations must be observed. Still, this viewer envisions being able to do laps in five of the pools, a surprisingly high number, given that most suburbanites do not care for pools with uniformed dimensions, which would reinforce in their mind the idea that a pool is for exercising rather than lounging beside. This might be why only the two smallest pools presented by Ruscha reflect what we associate with the look of a backyard pool. The smaller of the two— and of all the nine pools—is oval-shaped, with ladders at both ends. It doesn't appear to be very deep. Its dull and diminutive design seems to suggest that the homeowners cared more about just having a pool than using it, though the soda machine and cheap outdoor furniture visible in the photograph might suggest otherwise.

While a private outdoor pool and those who get to enjoy it can be hidden from the public, this is even more true in the case of indoor private pools. Some gym companies, like *24 Hour Fitness* and others, have built many of their facilities so that the pool and the lap swimmers appear visible to passersby on the street outside, but that is more the exception than the rule, as far as dense urban environments go. Take, for example, the private pools featured in "Beneath the Surface: A Peek at Private Pools," a *New York Times* article from September 2, 2022. Summers on the East Coast are about the beach, lakes, and ponds—think the New Jersey shore or the kettle ponds of Cape Cod. But after Labor Day, when temperatures begin to dip, most people in the NYC area have no choice but to go back to swimming indoors. Access to these facilities is limited, however—unless of course your building comes equipped with "a hidden realm most will never know: subterranean natatoria carved into basement floors and exquisitely maintained so residents can swim year-round—fall, winter, spring, summer.[2]

The choice of words—"natatoria" instead of "pools"— speaks to the uncommonness of these places, of course, but also to their rarified pedigree. Just scanning the images of the various facilities, one is stuck by how un-utilitarian they look. With the surrounding walls displaying original artworks and the light fixtures chosen by someone with a master's in interior design, the spaces look more like spas than exercise rooms. In many cases—with the exception, perhaps, of a tower in NoMad, where a lifeguard is on staff— the pools are so pristine and curated to the point of absurdity that they seem to be part of a staging ground for a cleansing ritual, places where one goes to escape not only the hustle and bustle of a city purported to never sleep, but also (let's be honest) their fellow, and less fortunate, New Yorkers. That most of the pools are not conducive to serious lap-swimming further reinforces their purpose as quiet spaces, where someone gets to be alone with their thoughts while, as one of the paragraphs suggests, wearing or not wearing a swimsuit.

Indeed, the idea of getting closer to oneself and to nature seems to be embedded in the design of the saltwater pool in a condo building in downtown Brooklyn. "The architectural rigor and lack of ornamentation are kind of monastic," says Katherine Newman, the designer, though her design also includes Casablanca granite walls with celestial cutouts.[3] I wonder what the former competitive high school swimmer who, we are told, swims about 44 laps—a lap measures 65 feet—on each visit to the pool, thinks about the motif. Does it make him feel like he's swimming outdoors at night? I also wonder what the air is like in this and the other pools, including the smaller ones, located in townhouses. Anyone who's ever swam or taken swim lessons in an old indoor pool, where the ceiling appeared touchable to anyone six-feet or taller, will forever associate such places with muggy air and eye-watering chlorine smell. Presumably, the occupants of the buildings pay exorbitant HOA fees, but that itself does not guarantee that the buildings come with state-of-the-art ventilation systems. There are, of course, indoor pools in places like Florida and California, but the opportunity to swim outdoors year-round is, in the case of the Golden State, part of the sunshine tax many of its residents are willing to pay.

It goes without saying that in the United States, the issue of class—education and occupation as well as financial means—continues to be intertwined with that of race and ethnicity. No area of life remains immune to its corrosive misalignment, so it shouldn't surprise anyone that leisure and recreation, understood as both the availability of time to play, or to do nothing, and of access to appropriate facilities, has been afforded some and withheld from others.

Writing in "America's Playground: Recreation and Race," his contribution to the anthology *A Companion to Los Angeles*, Lawrence Culver notes a shift in attitudes toward the issue of race and recreation in the 1920s. Apparently, in the early twentieth century, the city's pools were integrated, but for "segregationists, public bathing was a potentially explosive issue, mixing issues of race, gender, and the body in disturbing ways."[4] Consequently, while the mixing of genders was eventually allowed at the city's pools—and not just in LA but elsewhere in the US as well—"for some whites, the prospect of males and females of different races swimming together in revealing swimming attire was unacceptable."[5] In 1927, four years after the public pools were segregated, "a group of African Americans asked that the Los Angeles City Council appoint an African American to the City Parks Commission, no doubt hoping to end racist policies. Their request was denied."[6] And that wasn't the only move on the part of the white majority that added insult to injury. The city's Playground Department, which in its publications—pamphlets, brochures—used to depict children of different races and ethnicities playing together, including swimming together, changed course and ceased to feature Black children in its materials, literally erasing them. "The reason for this remains unclear," according to Culver, "but it seems likely that whites in Los Angeles were influenced by both national and local trends that were manifested in recreational policy."[7] Indeed, it wasn't just Black people who were leaving the South for the West, especially during the so-called "Great Migration," but whites too. Some of them aimed to apply their old ways—including racists and prejudiced views—in their new surroundings.

The story of how Blacks and whites were allowed to intermingle at recreational facilities—until they weren't, that is—played out across the country. In Pittsburgh, PA, for instance, the status quo ended in the summer of 1931, when the city opened a large outdoor pool in the Highland Park neighborhood. Similarly to Los Angeles, the spark came from the decision to allow males and females to swim together, to which white swimmers responded with violence. "On one occasion, a dozen black teenagers braved a barrage of racial epithets and entered the enormous pool only to have white swimmers start throwing rocks at them and then swarm them like human piranhas—punching and dunking them without mercy."[8] To make matters worse, several of the teens were arrested by a police officer on duty at the pool and charged with provoking a riot. As it turns out, this was just the beginning of pool segregation in Pittsburgh. While initially a decision was made to segregate the races only at those facilities where men and women crossed paths, eventually the white community employed intimidation and violence so extensively that the African Americans were limited to making use of just one facility.[9]

As University of Montana historian Jeff Wiltse observes, it wasn't until the Second World War that efforts to desegregate Pittsburgh's pools began to gain traction. While there were plenty of recalcitrant whites who did not see a contradiction in America's fight against tyranny abroad and Blacks being discriminated against en masse at home, there were others who did, and they began to agitate for the city's officials to desegregate facilities. This in turn empowered Black community leaders and citizens to undertake direct-action protests by, for instance, attempting to gain entrance to the Highland Park swimming pool. These protests didn't yield any meaningful progress, mainly because the Black community not only had to struggle against the prejudice of ordinary white citizens, but also the police and the elective officials, many of whom preached desegregation but in reality, turned a blind eye to the ongoing harassment of Black people at the city's pools.

In the summer of 1951, when Alexander Allen, the executive secretary of the local Urban League, tried but was prevented from swimming at the Highland Park pool, the local chapter of NAACP filed a lawsuit. Aware of the uphill battle that their arguments would face, the NAACP lawyers not only charged the city's officials with failing to protect African Americans at a public facility, but also called for the pool to be closed. Facing an even greater upheaval should the court order the closure of the pool, the city officials relented. Soon after, additional police officers—including, for the first time, Black officers—were assigned to the pool and tasked with protecting Black swimmers, who, with time, gained enough confidence to return to the Highland Park pool and, in 1953, after yet more protests, to another facility. Still, these were just two of the city's many facilities. As Jeff Wiltse poignantly reminds us, "The triumphs of 1951 and 1953 allowed African Americans safe access to a few municipal pools but did not alter the basic pattern of racial interactions—blacks and whites still mostly swam in separate pools."[10] What's more, in the ensuing years and decades, whites chose to vote with their feet. Not only did their actions contribute to an increase in geographical and residential segregation, but they also curtailed access to leisure and recreation for all Americans. As we have seen, many white residents chose to build pools in their backyards rather than share the lanes with their erstwhile Black neighbors.

Moreover, the white flight to the suburbs increased competition over urban space in general. Affluent whites not only built backyard pools but also sought recreational opportunities that smacked of exclusivity. The country club or a fitness gym charging exorbitant membership costs became their preferred sites for exercising and socializing. According to historian Victoria W. Wolcott, this change was reflected in the difference in legal structures between the North and the South. For instance, rather than seeing a "Whites Only" sign ("the universal symbol of Jim Crow") posted at the entrance, "a northern migrant would often encounter a 'Members

Only' sign."[11] This tactic allowed the white proprietors to stay within the law while still excluding Blacks on "personal grounds." But what's truly emblematic of how the desire for exclusivity among whites changed the landscape of cities' urban cores and led to the disuse of the recreational facilities located within them is the decline of the urban amusement park at the expense of the theme park. As Wolcott observes, "Disneyland, which opened in 1955, was the first and most successful American theme park. Its success premised on its dissociation from cities, in stark contrast to the traditional urban amusement parks like Buffalo's Crystal Beach."[12]

Watching Olympic swimming events on TV, it's hard not to notice that the sport is extremely white, notwithstanding the opening preliminary heats, in which slower swimmers, many of whom hail from African and Caribbean nations, compete. But the lack of racial diversity is also apparent in the US, where African Americans "are enormously underrepresented in the top tiers of American swimmers, despite all the black success in other sports."[13] Sadly, this disparity is underscored by drowning statistics. According to the Centers for Disease Control (CDC),

> Drowning death rates for Black people are 1.5 times higher than the rates for White people. Disparities are highest among Black children ages 5-9 (rates 2.6 times higher) and ages 10-14 (rates 3.6 times higher). In swimming pools, Black children ages 10-14 years drown at rates 7.6 times higher than White children.[14]

What we in the United States refer to as white flight has its correlatives around the world. In countries with more racially homogenous populations, such as Greece, the discussion of who gets to swim and where is rooted in class and material status. As the authors of one recent study argue, "pools can be considered a proxy of increased social-spatial disparities reflecting class segregation and economic polarization at the local scale." Discussing the urbanization of the entire Mediterranean Europe and not just Greece, the authors observe a movement of populations not only away from city centers and into the suburbs, but more specifically into what they refer to as a "lock-living" style. These proliferating gated communities come with properties built on larger parcels, with the swimming pool being their key feature, thus contributing to segregation and "spatial homogenization."[15] It is no surprise that these communities attract higher income earners—that's the case the world over—but it is to the authors' credit that they also make the connection between the density of swimming pools and the area's higher use of resources in general. In regions with a warm climate—like the Athens metropolitan region, for instance, where by 2015 nearly 10,000 pools were in operation—swimming pools are sought-after for the relief they offer during hot summer months, but their colossal drain on the power grid and water usage cannot be understated.

Anecdotal evidence suggests, however, that as much as some people pine for a backyard oasis of their own—and the pool's shape (think the guitar or the cowboy boot) reflects their owner's whims and quirks—others are looking for ways to get rid of their swimming pool. In arid regions, including Southwestern United States, the fight over already-scare water is only going to intensify. Filling in a pool with dirt costs a lot less than maintaining it year-round.

Drained swimming pools are a strange sight, even after the last of the water, some of which seems to remain in the pool's lowest spot for a long time, is gone. Their provenance and purpose makes swimming pools hard to imagine as anything other than, well, swimming pools; but on the other hand empty swimming pools remind us of so much more. They are buildings flipped upside down, in a way, their highest points buried underground. Or the opposite: they are buildings, perhaps warehouses, with their rooftops blown off by time and disuse. The markings on their walls, such as "Deep End" or "8 ft," when severed from their context, force us to imagine the pools as they existed in their previous life, full of water and patrons, or perhaps a lap swimmer, who picked the wrong time to do his exercising and consequently had to dodge children chasing a beachball.

Pools that have been emptied due to wartime activities are particularly striking. Their diving towers, rising against the landscape, resemble a sketchy design of something that could've found its place in a sci-fi film or novel. Or take their gaping drains. When I look at them, I think of Andrzej Wajda's *Kanał* (1957), a film which depicts the tragedy of the 1944 Warsaw Uprising, particularly the part of it that forced insurgents and civilians to use the city's sewer system to escape German encirclements. The drains in an empty pool, both covered with a grate or uncovered, stare back at me while I wonder where they lead to or if anyone ever tried to hide something, anything inside them. Certainly, the drains are not large enough for a person to squeeze through, even though that fact alone has never stopped a child worrying about being sucked into one while swimming in his family's backyard pool, but the surroundings walls, chipped and pockmarked with bullets, make the mind go there nonetheless. It's a good thing, then, that children find ways to play in those empty pools and not be scared, kicking a soccer ball against the walls, chasing after it as if the empty pool were a giant pinball machine.

In a similar vein but in a different context, on a bad surf day, surfers exchange one board for another and hunt for a smooth piece of concrete, sometimes violating trespassing and private property laws in the process, which seems to be part of the allure. In the early 1960s, after the skateboarding community began to organize itself by holding competitions, the sport's popularity grew immensely—but so did its scrutiny by public officials who were concerned with what must have been a skyrocketing number of injuries and thus visits to emergency rooms. In fact, as the author Cole Louison reminds us, in 1965 "skateboarding was declared 'a new menace' by the California Medical Association."[16]

Hopping over a fence and skateboarding in a drained pool must seem as exciting today as it did in the '60s or '70s, when new technologies, mainly the invention of the urethane wheel, enabled skateboarders to attempt ever more daring tricks. The speed of a rider gliding at gravity-defining angles along a pool's smooth walls became even more thrilling when the rider realized he could launch himself into the air. What made all this possible to some extent was Mother Nature. In the 1970s, many LA homeowners drained their pools to account for a prolonged drought, and these "concrete oases"—as Tyler Stallings calls them in his article, "From Beefcake to Skatecake: Shifting Depictions of Masculinity and the Backyard Swimming Pool in Southern California"[17]— attracted riders from all over, including the now-legendary members of the Z-Boys surfing team founded in Venice Beach in 1973. "The Z-Boys took their surf style of skating and their attitude of treating urban landscape like their personal playground to the empty pools."[18] But what made their escapades famous were the articles and photographs that Craig Stecyk published in the magazine *SkateBoarder*.

As Stallings sees it, trespassing to skate in an empty pool isn't just about stepping onto someone's property, "but also into the privacy and security of the nuclear family. Even though this notion suggests a provision for criminal acts, it also represents an act of rebellion against the traditional, rational-grid plan of cities."[19] The notion of what is rational and irrational, and therefore possible or not possible, lies at the heart of every counterculture movement aiming to push the boundaries of acceptable behavior. The same logic applies to sports, especially the sports popularized by the arrival of the X-Games in 1994. Skateboarding, BMX riding, and similar disciplines not only came to define what extreme sports are, but their stars also influenced scores of viewers in how to dress and behave in ways that suggested that going against the grain and cultivating an air of brashness or insouciance about oneself was perfectly normal.

Writing in a 1975 *SkateBoarder* article, Craig Stecyk conflates the skater's desire for autonomy with pushing for and establishing new limits, when he writes that "You can go as far as you want to take it, or perhaps more aptly as far as it takes you. After you leave the realm of traditional preconceptions, you enter the area of endless freedom. There exists no right or wrong, rules are unheard of, and the course is uncharted."[20] However, this push toward the new and the undiscovered is necessarily also a kind of return. Today we are used to seeing selfies everywhere, in print and online, and the Z-Boys and other skaters likewise posed for the camera with eagerness. Some of it stemmed from a desire to see their fleeting moves documented, or, after breaking onto someone's property, being immortalized in a transgressive act. What's more, the wish to embody and project autonomy through dress or behavior only highlighted the fact that the riders were irrevocably tethered to and dependent on their bodies. As Stallings puts it, "When skateboarders photographed each other and circulated these images to their readers of the magazines they put into practice a self-reflexivity that redefined masculinity."[21] Indeed, looking at Stecyk's images, we are exposed to men—where are the women, one might ask?—whose wiry yet toned bodies and long, sun-bleached hair are the norm. Another thing that's common to the images is that they suggest a comradery shared by the skaters.

These connections—physical, material, or spiritual—are not incidental. A body moving through space will always be connected to its environment, even while it is redefining it. Thus, riding around the bowl of an empty pool, a skateboarder comes to represent both the end of a dream—that of a backyard oasis—and the beginning of a new one through a reincorporation of that space into the social fabric of which it is a part. Additionally, if we focus on the men's physique, especially the body contortions that make athletic moves possible, and add the element of water to it, then we might end up, as Stallings suggests, with the pool resembling something akin to a womb. In Stecyk's photographs, then, the appropriation of the swimming pools "suggests an active process of rebirth."[22] As such, the process is full of painful reevaluation of one's identity while also being generative as far as achieving autonomy is concerned. Whether or not this leads to lasting self-realization is anyone's guess, but there is no doubt that skateboarding in a drained pool—or along drainage pipes and aqueducts and creeks with concrete embankments, for that matter—has helped countless people improve their self-esteem and redefine their relationship to the rest of society. Indeed, as architectural historian Iain Borden sees it, the attraction that "pools, ditches and full-pipes" held for skateboarders is in their "appearance as second nature." He goes on: "That these constructions were commonly located in the wastelands, deserts and forgotten spaces of the city was a condition which imbued them with an archaeological character—they appeared to be primeval material elements since forgotten by the inhabitants of the city."[23]

While sneaking into properties to skate in drained pools seems like a thing of the past, skateboarders nevertheless still crave the experience. Some of them grew up watching *Lords of Dogtown* (2005), an entertaining mishmash of biographical drama and the story of how skateboarding shed its counterculture roots and became a sport with a worldwide fanbase. In the film, the eponymous group of skaters is shown driving around neighborhoods posher than their Venice/south Santa Monica base and using binoculars to spot empty backyard pools. The thrill of finding such a place is palpable; the risk of getting caught—in a few scenes we see the trespassers getting chased by angry homeowners and their dogs—is clearly an important part of the experience.

For those not keen on breaking the law, there is the Pink Motel in Sun Valley, California, which has been used for a setting in countless movies and TV productions, including now-classic skateboarding films such as the 1987 *The Search for Animal Chin* by Stacy Peralta whose own rise to fame was depicted in *Lords of Dogtown*. Peralta's film starred young Tony Hawk and other members of The Bones Brigade skateboarding team. The Pink Motel, which was built in 1946 and no longer serves visitors driving across the San Fernando Valley, plays hosts to the Pink Motel Shred Fest, a skateboarding competition that also features live music, art, and all sorts of skateboarding merchandise. It is the place where countless up-and-coming skaters can run into legends of the sport, while for those who can't make it to the festival, the pool, in the shape of a fish, can be rented filled or drained. The palm trees are gratis.

* * *

Sports and social advocacy do mix well, and not just in the world of skateboarding. Swimming, for instance, may strike us as an activity one performs to tune out the world, but that's not how Mao Zedong saw it. A lifelong swimmer, Zedong cultivated the image of himself as a strong athlete to burnish his political credentials and, even more importantly, to appear God-like to the Chinese people. When it became clear to everyone that his Great Leap Forward was a catastrophic mishap, stymying China's development and leading to the death of millions of people, his grip on power began to be seen as a liability even by those in his inner circle.

The ensuing infighting led Mao Zedong, on July 16, 1966, to take part in the 11th annual Cross-Yangtze swim competition as a way of broadcasting to his opponents that his vitality hadn't waned and that he remained strong enough to lead the country. "Surrounded by six swimming bodyguards, accompanied by giant portraits of himself and by placards asking for 10,000 years of life for him," Zedong stayed in the water for over an hour, allegedly covering nearly ten miles in that time.[24] Whether he covered that distance is beside the point—in fact, even with a very strong current his pace would've been faster than what we see at the Olympics—because what mattered most in any case were the optics.

With over 5000 other swimmers participating, Zedong's dip in the Yangtze at Wuhan was a propagandist's dream come true—and it set the murderous Cultural Revolution in motion. To the dismay of his opponents, "Mao's swim on July 16 showed a man who was in motion, both physically, as he swam in China's largest river, and geographically, as he made his way toward Beijing."[25] The symbolism of Zedong's stunt wasn't lost on anyone. Soon after, "Mao was returned to power, and he and his supporters wielded that power recklessly and ruthlessly for the better part of a decade. And Mao moved his official residence to the building in Zhongnanhai that housed the indoor swimming pool."[26] As if that weren't enough of a residence-change, he had his bedroom set up inside what was once the facility's changing room. Zedong swam daily in the 50-meter pool for the rest of his life.[27]

During those ten years following the Yangtze swim and preceding his death in September 1976, he continued to extol the benefits of swimming not just to his subordinates but also to world leaders, not unlike in August 1958, when Zedong proposed to the visiting leader of the Soviet Union, Nikita Khrushchev, that they meet at the pool and go swimming together. Did the Chinese leader know beforehand that Khrushchev couldn't swim? According to various sources, the interpreters stayed on deck and followed the two leaders as they swam or, in the case of Khrushchev, floated up and down the pool. The Soviet leader later recalled, "Well, I got sick of it . . . I crawled out, sat on the edge, and dangled my legs in the pool. Now I was on top and he was swimming below."[28] I bet the Chinese leader and the Chinese people would beg to differ.

AFTERWORD

FROM POOL TO PAGE

"2 (August 1914) Germany has declared war on
Russia.—Swimming school in the afternoon."[1]

—FRANZ KAFKA

I am shifting through memories, stored on the hard drive
inside my head, for the first pool I ever splashed in. Was
it one of the outdoor long-course pools that half of my
hometown frequented during summer months? Or was it
something much smaller, a hotel pool, perhaps, or a pool at
the resort owned by the company one of my parents worked
for when I was in preschool? Company-owned resorts were
a big deal in the People's Republic of Poland. Though they
offered basic accommodations—picture flimsy huts and
a larger cinderblock building where everyone took their
meals—free employee vouchers enabled countless families to

go on vacation every year. When I flip through my parents' photo album, with pictures taken on trips to the mountains or lakes, I see a cherubic kid raising hell with buckets and sand toys, but no swimming pool, alas, though that's not surprising. Unlike other countries in the former Eastern Bloc, not to mention places like Iceland, which, according to Tsui, "is one of the world's leaders in swimming pools per capita" (and even created a special road sign for it: "a head poking out of two rows of blue waves,") Poland has never been known for its swimming facilities, let alone the number of them.[2]

Then it must have been the outdoor facility I've mentioned, where the water was milky-green, making it impossible to see anything beneath the surface. Its popularity stemmed, at least in part, from the fact that hardly anyone owned a car in those days, which made getting to local lakes or rivers difficult. It also represented recreation on the cheap. All that was needed was several blankets to spread out on the grassy areas adjacent to the pools—a deep one, with a diving board, a shallow one, plus a children's wading pool—and something to eat, usually tomato or cucumber sandwiches, a bag of pretzel sticks, and lots of suntanning lotion. That's right—skin cancer wasn't part of the conversation back then.

I remember jumping into the arms of my half-submerged dad or his twin brother, doggy paddling back to the wall, climbing out, and doing it again. And again. And again. The pool wasn't heated, but I, like kids the world over, did not mind the cold water; in fact, it was impossible to get me away from the pool. I love sliced tomato or cucumber on bread, and chunks of watermelon—another summer staple—to this day, but back then I would sooner turn into a shivering prune than take a break.

I don't remember if the pool, which was made of rough concrete, was divided into sections for those who knew how to swim and those who didn't, but years later, in elementary school, I would visit the pool with my buddies on most summer days. What did we do? We played tag—and not just any tag, but what we called "corner tag." While the person who was "it" treaded water, everyone else's goal was to dive or jump in and swim across the corner, where the pool's two walls formed a right angle, and get out of the water before being tagged. Because we didn't always play this game in the deep end, there were plenty of visits to the lifeguard stand for treatment of bloody noses or scraped knees. After 1989, which marked the end of communism in Poland, the aquatics complex would fall into disuse along with countless similar facilities across the country, thanks to the so-called shock therapy aimed at transitioning the country from a centralized to a capitalist economy. With state funding disappearing overnight, the pools became home to ducks and geese. Eventually the facility reopened, although with just one pool, and only to close again soon after. Luckily, someone else has since put some money into it and now the place is once again open during July and August.

I didn't learn how to swim there, or not exactly, but the pool near the man-made lake in Kraków's Nowa Huta district gave me the first taste of how getting from point A to point B in the pool can change one's life.

It has also given me a lifelong appreciation for those who teach swim lessons and those who take them, especially later in life. Indeed, today, as a former competitive swimmer, I greatly admire the adult novice swimmers I see at the pool. They often get involved in swimming because their children are taking lessons, and—in case the family decides to take that beachside vacation they've been putting off—they too want to be water safe. Or perhaps they've been told that swimming won't be as hard on their joints as running, and now they start in the shallow end, doing the breaststroke with their heads above water, right next to the wall. Or perhaps being in the water just makes them feel good. According to some researchers, "swimming can produce the release of endorphins and endocannabinoids (the brain's natural cannabis-like substances), which reduce the brain's response to stress and anxiety. . . . In swimming, the muscles are constantly stretching and relaxing in a rhythmic manner, and this movement is accompanied by deep, rhythmic breathing, all of which help to put swimmers into a quasi-meditative state."[3] Doesn't that sound divine? Furthermore, if they become regulars, I eventually see them try to do the backstroke, which means a lot of coughing and sneezing, since they haven't yet learned how to keep the water from going up their nose. While their awkwardness in the water slowly turns to proficiency, I offer suggestions for fixing their strokes; for example, how to breathe to the side in freestyle. In short, I become a fan, and sympathize with these amateurs, slowly making their way through uncharted waters, because I too changed courses midstream, having more or less abandoned competitive swimming for poetry.

There is a tendency to believe, not without some basis, that jocks stay jocks, and that poets are born, not made. As such, my journey from world swimming rankings to the pages of literary journals is unusual. I became a serious swimmer (i.e., one that trained two times per day, twelve times per week) when I was nine or ten, after I'd been recruited to join the local team following a year of taking swim lessons. In those days, swim lessons were a mandatory part of physical education in communist Poland. Once a week, instead of running around the perimeter of the gym, jumping over the hobble horse, or learning how to play basketball, we marched to the local swimming pool, an indoor facility that was, and is to this day, a far cry from the Olympic-caliber pools I would later encounter. That local pool was a standard twenty-five meters in length but had only three lanes (later, hooks for an extra lane line were installed, thus adding an extra lane by hanging the lane lines closer together). Both boys and girls were required to wear white swimsuits. We blew bubbles a lot. Then, after a year of perfecting the freestyle and backstroke, the more promising among us were invited to join the team, which included transferring to another school.

All along, my swimming friends and I had to take classes just like all primary school students. The ones I remember best were classes in Polish language and literature. Our brilliant teacher for all five years, Ms. K., made certain

FIGURE 3 Photo by Aleksander Romański.

that we spoke and wrote in good Polish and were able to name and explain the seven cases for nouns, pronouns, and adjectives. She also introduced us to Polish poetry, and I began to write my first poems. Did we read Czesław Miłosz? I don't remember. Did we read Adam Mickiewicz? Yes—there was no getting around his epic poem *Pan Tadeusz*. Zbigniew Herbert? Yes—who could forget lines like these: "in the second year of the war / our biology teacher was killed / by history's schoolyard bullies"?[4] The enthusiasm and dedication of Ms. K., who worked tirelessly to expand our chlorine-smudged horizons, was nothing short of inspiring—although the poetry didn't immediately take root. Little did I know that those first inauspicious lessons helped shape who I am today.

But before I decided to give poetry a chance, I had more swimming and racing to do. Although I'd been successful on both the national and European junior scene, my first big break came in 1994. During the summer of that year, I represented Poland at the European Junior Championships in Pardubice in the Czech Republic. I remember talking with my teammates about the famous horse racetrack en route to the event, but the only racing we did was in the pool—a beautiful facility with a separate diving well—where I came in fourth in two races, which was good enough to score an invitation to come to the United States for a year of training in Southern California. It was the opportunity of a lifetime, and my coach and parents knew it. I landed at LAX in the first days of September 1994. I'll never forget my first glimpse of the clear-blue sky, the palm trees, the many car models and makes cruising the freeways and wide boulevards. Seeing backyard pools at my teammates' houses made me believe I was in heaven.

But it didn't take very long for the homesickness to set in. Not only did I hardly speak a word of English, but I also missed everything Polish, including being able to read and speak in my native tongue. The highly structured, not to mention exhausting, workout regimen, which included getting up at 4 a.m. for the morning workout and swimming an average ten miles each day, didn't do much to alleviate my sense of having been uprooted and tossed into the deep end of an existential crisis. Not surprisingly, I was just an okay high school student, but even though I had only recently gained a working knowledge of English, I did markedly better in English and history than math and science courses, just as I had in Poland. When the news came that my fellowship would be renewed for another year because my times kept getting faster, I celebrated, but I could also sense that something was coming to an end—that my interests were shifting toward the arts, and toward literature in particular.

Reading poetry in another language wasn't easy, especially since the internet and electronic dictionaries weren't yet widely available. I still have a journal I kept during those days. Its pages are filled with lines written in Polish by someone who missed his parents and friends, but also began to accept the possibility of staying in the US for college. The slightly faded lined pages also include my first attempts at poetic expression in English. Many of these poems are quiet in tone, showing how the author struggled to hide his impoverished command of English, if only from himself. The few interesting lines found in the journal are marked by my striving for clarity, and especially attention to details, most of which were collected on occasional walks through Orange County suburbia, where I stayed with a loving host family. This urban impressionism reveals not so much my desire for self-expression, but rather a wish to penetrate and translate the foreignness I felt vis-à-vis my surroundings. I wrote long letters home in Polish, but I was writing more and more poems—bad ones—that spoke of someone fumbling for the light switch in the dark, someone trying to connect his internal feelings and thoughts with the outside world. I wasn't quite like the speaker of Robert Pinsky's melodious "Samurai Song," who says that "When I had no roof I made / Audacity my roof," but I too wanted to be that strong, independent, and confident.[5]

By the time I entered college on a swimming scholarship, I had accepted the fact that random words or even complete verses would slosh around in my head during workouts. It might be true that, as linguists tell us, an average person needs only about two hundred words to communicate with others and survive from day to day; but that wasn't enough for me. My aspiration toward poetry was synonymous with my desire to improve my English, which, after three years of high school, sufficed for basic self-expression, but hadn't yet approached the level where I could utilize its famously extensive vocabulary. So I memorized words, and I read everything I could get my hands on. I had reasons to be discouraged—I almost failed both introductions to English and American literature courses—but I persisted, just as I had in the pool over the years. I even read Miłosz in English, since I couldn't get my hands on a good Polish edition of his poems; this embarrassed and fascinated me in equal measure. Indeed, the Polish poets I read in translation— Miłosz, Herbert, Szymborska, Zagajewski— allowed me to regain a sense of belonging to a particular place, if not a particular time. It was as if their translated poems hadn't lost their original Polish register, allowing me to tap into the frequency I had tuned out in my quest to dull the pangs of homesickness and to feel at home in the US.

After several years of reading nothing but Polish poets—first in translation, then, when the world seemed to get a lot smaller with the advent of the internet and exchanging books between Poland and the US became less impractical—I began to tire of the historical context that marks much of Polish poetry in the twentieth century. Acting as a de facto ambassador for the Polish poets, I also wanted to spread the word about those Poles who wrote about their daily lives. Consequently, reading Miłosz's "Dedication," I thought more about poetry as a source of nourishment and salvation than as a conduit for historical information. As we know, Miłosz was against the 1944 Warsaw Uprising, which his famous poem references by way of addressing the perished young poets and the rest of the young Polish intelligentsia, and I urged my American friends to look beyond the "poetry of witness" aspect of his and other poets' work. Adam Zagajewski and his New Wave friends—including Julian Kornhauser, whom I ended up translating—excited me the most at that time, when I searched for a way to find meaning in my life as a swimmer who continued to swim in order to keep his full scholarship. Like the speaker in many of Adam Zagajewski's poems, I too oscillated between ecstasy and doubt in my daily life. Though I swam in a chlorinated pool rather than a sea, I felt alone, but not lonely, repeating these lines from "On Swimming":

I love to swim in the sea, which keeps
talking to itself

in the monotone of a vagabond
who no longer recalls
exactly how long he's been on the road.

It took me a long time to do so, but I've come to accept the possibility that swimming is "like prayer: palms join and part, / join and part, / almost without end."[6]

Eventually, I began to read American poets, many of whom were a joy to discover. Not surprisingly, given the fact that he'd translated Miłosz's work, I read Robert Hass—and must have read and reread his "The Lament for the Poles of Buffalo" a hundred times, quietly repeating to myself the ending of the poem's first section,

Mr. Lewandowski, Mrs. Slominsky,
I toss hard words at you
from here on Chestnut Ridge,
white Anglo-Saxon words,
heavy, strange as buckshot
on the tongues of your grandfathers."[7]

The poem captivated me. It captured the tragedy of the immigrant experience. Surely Hass, a Californian, saw himself no less out of place in Buffalo than the Polish immigrants whom he taught. Reading this poem now, I think of Buffalo as how I saw it when I traveled there for a swimming competition during one winter of my high school years. I'd seen snow once before since moving to America, in Seattle, but that's what I remember enjoying the most about the Upstate city—the snow and the harsh, angular architecture of its downtown. The snow reminded me of Poland, of course, but Hass's poem and the work that had gone into building up the downtown area, which at the time seemed in dire need of a makeover, made me contemplate how much of our collective human experience is really about finding the most suitable way to express ourselves, so that others can learn about themselves.

Indeed, while the general view of swimming and other sports hinges on the assumption that all athletes strive to do their best before the world, poetry isn't all that different: in moments of private contemplation, poets long to be in the world rather than to shy away from it. The only, and most important, distinction between the two solitary activities lies in the fact that poetry is not a race, that it cannot be timed or measured, and, as such, it is paradoxically much less individualistic than the pursuit of athletic glory. In a country like the United States, where the model of civil solidarity has not been tested by centuries of significant external pressure, most Americans think of poetry as a vehicle for narcissistic peregrinations; yet poetry's communal reach is much wider. Poetry cannot and should not be reduced to a mouthpiece for causes and agendas, but by reading it, we acknowledge the interconnectedness of our private joys and fears. Is that not what Elizabeth Bishop's masterpieces "The End of March" and "In the Waiting Room" teach us? Bishop might have been the most private and reticent of our poets, but she expressed her sense of alienation with such great skill and casual offhandedness that any reader can share it—and thereby overcome it. Poetry remains the best place to turn to for a nuanced view of life.

During my junior and senior years of college, I stayed up late reading Eliot, then had to crawl out of bed and put myself through physical and emotional pain in order to prepare for another swim meet that always seemed to lie just over the horizon. But I couldn't get "The Waste Land" out of my head, nor could I stop thinking about Louise Glück's "Mock Orange" or Paul Muldoon's "Incantata." I swam butterfly down the pool, wondering why the speaker of "Mock Orange" hated the smell of the orange tree blossoms so much, while on the way back, gasping for breath, I thought about the rhyme scheme of the Irish poet's great elegy, his romanticism and anguish—"that you might reach out, arrah, / and take in your ink-stained hands my own hands stained with ink"[8]—that come bubbling to the surface not in spite of, but because of his superb technique. The two views of life—one more tragic than the other—in Wallace Stevens's "The Emperor of Ice Cream," expressed with such matter-of-factness, as if the poet had wanted to eliminate any possibility of second thoughts that would only require him to keep revisiting the misery that was his private life, made me want to escape my own quotidian stomping ground.

One just can't be a poet and serious athlete at the same time—one must choose one over the other. Why? Well, serious athletics requires complete dedication. When it comes to reaping the benefits of all the hard work, one can't be distracted by other endeavors and risk losing focus—after all, there is a reason why a certain company's marketing slogan reads "Just do it." At the same time, poetry entails long contemplation, the obsessive nature of choosing words because one either sounds better than the other or works in other surprising ways, connoting something that no other word could. That's dedication of a different sort, but it is no less complete. What's more, swimming is all about getting to the wall first; indeed, it's such a tough sport because of its unyielding competitive atmosphere. On the other hand, a working poet may have ideas of greatness, but most of us admit that we are engaged in a conversation, be it with our predecessors, our contemporaries, ourselves, or the world at large. Moreover, this conversation cannot be solely about poetry, but must include other arts and disciplines whose impact on our views and ideas may not be immediately apparent. While my own desire to learn and speak English like a native speaker may have something to do with my wish to put an end to my getting picked on, or being called an alien by the funnier of my peers, now that I realize how difficult it is to write a successful poem, I want to write one again and again, even if only to "fail better" each time.

Eventually, poetry and literature won the battle over the jock. Indeed, I didn't always have "the killer instinct" necessary to get the job done in the pool. Too much of a dabbler, I was much more interested in the why than the how, and my interests quickly outgrew the confines of the pool. It was only with time that I came to wonder if perhaps swimming and writing poetry aren't that different. Among the few things they share, none matters more than the desire to go back in. In swimming, you come to the wall at the end of the lap and dip under the surface to do a flip-turn, and when writing a poem—whether it's your first or the one you've been trying to write all your life—you come to the end of the line, turn around, and do your best try to cover some of the distance all over again.

ACKNOWLEDGMENTS

Some of this material stems from conversations with family and friends, and I owe a great deal of gratitude to Emily Hodgson Anderson, Grant Klarich Johnson, Hubie Kerns, Zach Mann, Rada Owen, Kenneth Rippetoe, and Kevin A. Wisniewski for expanding my ideas about what a swimming pool is.

Thank you to G. Lofthus and Kasia Romańska (for Aleksander Romański's photo) for their photographs.

Many thanks to my fellow swimmers, especially members of the Southern California Aquatics (SCAQ) masters team, and to my coaches over the years and on two continents, for making the time in the pool grueling and fun at the same time.

Thanks also to my colleagues at the University of Washington, Seattle, for their support of my writings.

Huge thanks to the Object Lessons series editors, Chris and Ian, and to the entire team at Bloomsbury for embracing this project and guiding it into the world.

Special thanks to my wife, Dena, with whom I fell in love with at a pool, and to our children, Iza and Ed, for endowing my work with joy and purpose.

NOTES

Chapter 1

1 Teresa Rivas and Al Root, "This Swimming-Pool Stock Got a Big Covid Boost. Why It's Still Worth Buying," *Barron's Magazine*, December 28, 2020. https://www.barrons.com /articles/why-pool-corp-stock-is-still-a-buy51608821392 (accessed February 3, 2023).

2 Mara Gay, "Too Many New Yorkers Can't Swim. It's Time to Change That," *New York Times*, July 24, 2022. https://www .nytimes.com/2022/07/24/opinion/new-york-city-swimming -pools.html (accessed January 18, 2023).

3 Reiner Stach, *Kafka: The Early Years*, translated by Shelley Frisch (Princeton: Princeton UP, 2017), 105.

4 Ibid., 107.

Chapter 2

1 Francis Hodgson, *The Swimming Pool in Photography* (Berlin: Hatje Cantz Verlag, 2018), 10.

2 Lawrence Culver, "America's Playground: Recreation and Race," in *A Companion to Los Angeles*, ed. William Deverell and Greg Hise, (Chichester: Wiley-Blackwell, 2010), 433.

3 Hodgson, *The Swimming Pool in Photography*, 33.

4 Deanna Templeton, *The Swimming Pool* (Davenport: Um Yeah Arts, 2016).

5 Ed Templeton, afterword to *The Swimming Pool* (Davenport: Um Yeah Arts, 2016), n.p.

6 Robert Atkins, et al., *Backyard Oasis: The Swimming Pool in Southern California Photography*, 1945-1982 (Munich: Prestel, 2012), 128.

7 Helen Little, *Tate Introduction: David Hockney* (London: Tate Publishing, 2017), 15-16.

8 Marco Livingston, *David Hockney* (London: Thames & Hudson, 2017), 141.

Chapter 3

1 John Cheever, *Collected Stories and Other Writings*, edited by Blake Bailey (New York: Library of America, 2009), 726.

2 Ibid., 727.

3 Ibid., 728.

4 Ibid.

5 Ibid., 730.

6 Ibid., 731.

7 Ibid.

8 Ibid., 733.

9 Ibid., 737.

10 Ibid.

11 Howard Means, *Splash! 10,000 Years of Swimming* (New York: Hachette Books, 2020), 44.

12 Lynn Sherr, *Swim: Why We Love the Water* (New York: PublicAffairs, 2013), 110.

13 Means, *Splash! 10,000 Years of Swimming*, 44.

14 Vladimir Nabokov, *Novels 1955-1962: Lolita, Pnin, Pale Fire, Lolita: A Screenplay*, edited by Brian Boyd (New York: Library of America, 1996), 222.

15 Ibid., 222-223.

16 Walt Whitman, "I Sing the Body Electric," *Poetry Foundation*, https://www.poetryfoundation.org/poems/45472/i-sing-the-body-electric (accessed January 23, 2023).

17 Carl Philips, "Swimming," *Academy of American Poets*, https://poets.org/poem/swimming (accessed January 23, 2023).

18 Oliver Sacks, "Water Babies," *New Yorker*, May 19, 1997. https://www.newyorker.com/magazine/1997/05/26/water-babies, 45.

19 Ibid., 45.

20 Ibid.

21 *The Swimmers*, directed by Sally El-Hosaini (2020, Working Title), 2:15:31. https://www.netflix.com/watch/81365134.

Chapter 4

1 Robert Atkins et al, *Backyard Oasis*, 11.

2 Craig Kellogg, "Beneath the Surface: A Peak at Private Pools," New York Times, September 2, 2022, par. 2. https://www.nytimes.com/interactive/2022/09/02/realestate/luxury/new-york-indoor-private-pools.html (accessed January 25, 2023).

3   Craig Kellogg, "Beneath the Surface: A Peak at Private Pools," par. 4.

4   Culver, "America's Playground: Recreation and Race," 427.

5   Ibid., 427.

6   Ibid.

7   Ibid., 426.

8   Jeff Wiltse, "Swimming against Segregation: The Struggle to Desegregate." *Pennsylvania Legacies* 10, no. 2 (2010), 13. https://doi.org/10.5215/pennlega.10.2.0012)

9   Ibid., 14.

10 Ibid., 16.

11 Victoria W. Wolcott, *Race, Riots, and Roller Coasters: The Struggle Over Segregated Recreation in America* (Philadelphia: University of Pennsylvania Press, 2014), 19.

12 Ibid., 126.

13 Means, *Splash! 10,000 Years of Swimming*, 216.

14 "Drowning Facts" https://www.cdc.gov/drowning/facts/index.html (accessed January 25, 2023).

15 Margherita Carlucci et al, "Social-spatial Disparities and the Crisis: Swimming Pools as a Proxy of Class Segregation in Athens," Social Indicators Research (2022) 161, 937. https://doi.org/10.1007/s11205-020-02448-y

16 Cole Louison, *Impossible: Rodney Mullen, Ryan Sheckler, and the Fantastic History of Skateboarding* (Guilford: Lyons Press, 2011), 4.

17 Atkins et al, *Backyard Oasis*, 133.

18 Ibid.

19 Ibid., 133-134.

20 Ibid., 136.

21 Ibid., 137.

22 Ibid., 141.

23 Iain Borden, *Skateboarding, Space and the City: Architecture and the Body* (New York: Berg, 2001), 45.

24 Roger Hudson, "The Great Helmsman Goes Swimming," History Today, Volume 62 Issue 5 May 2012. https://www .historytoday.com/archive/focus/great-helmsman-goes -swimming (accessed January 25, 2023).

25 James Carter, "The Power of Symbolism: The Swim that Changed Chinese History," *The China Project*, https:// thechinaproject.com/2021/07/14/power-of-symbolism-the -swim-that-changed-chinese-history/ (accessed January 25, 2023).

26 Ibid.

27 Jung Chang and Jon Halliday, *Mao: The Unknown Story* (New York: Anchor, 2006), 549.

28 Ben Gaskin, "Swimming Pool Diplomacy: Khrushchev, Mao, and the Sino-Soviet Split," *On This Day in History*, https:// www.onthisday.com/articles/swimming-pool-diplomacy -khrushchev-mao-and-the-sino-soviet-split (accessed January 25, 2023).

Afterword

1 Franz Kafka, *The Diaries*, translated by Ross Benjamin (New York: Schocken Books, 2022), 285.

2 Bonnie Tsui, *Why We Swim* (Chapel Hill: Algonquin Books, 2020), 44.

3 Wallace J. Nichols, *Blue Mind: The Surprising Science That Shows How Being Near, In, On, or Under Water Can Make You Happier, Healthier, More Connected, and Better at What You Do* (New York: Back Bay Books, 2015), 110.

4 Zbigniew Herbert, *Collected Poems: 1956-1998*, translated and edited by Alissa Valles (New York: Ecco Press, 2008), 93.

5 Robert Pinsky, *Jersey Rain* (New York: Farrar, Straus & Giroux, 2000), 3.

6 Adam Zagajewski, *Without End: New and Selected Poems*, translated by Clare Cavanagh et al (New York: Farrar, Straus & Giroux, 2003), 273.

7 Robert Hass, *Field Guide* (New Haven: Yale University Press, 1973), 68.

8 Paul Muldoon, *New Selected Poems: 1968-1994* (London: Faber & Faber, 1996), 180.

INDEX

Stroller

The Best Books of 2022, *New Yorker*

 For Morgan, strollers aren't just tools we use, or products we buy; they're dense symbols, with no single or settled meaning, of our relationships to parenting."

—*The New Yorker*

Doll

 jaw dropping."

—*Is This Mutton?*

 [Hart's] observations about how dolls are emotional vectors—simultaneously objects of scorn and adoration—are revelatory and relatable."

—*Brevity*

 a fascinating personal and public exploration of the deeper meanings behind the plastic, polymer, and porcelain playthings that still shape American girlhood."

—Susan Shapiro, New York Times bestselling author of *Unhooked, Five Men Who Broke My Heart, and Barbie: Sixty Years of Inspiration*

Doll is a heartfelt, intimate, and clever study of objects
that terrify some and thrill others... giving us new
perspective on these tiny, fragile mirrors."

—Allison Horrocks, co-host of the *Dolls of Our
Lives* (formerly titled *American Girls Podcast*)

Sewer

Get ready to dive into the wondrous underworld of
waste. . . . It's perfect for the fatberg fan in your life."

—*Mental Floss*

Hester goes deep on a topic that few relish[–]the inner
workings of wastewater infrastructure—all to answer
questions of how human habits are reshaping the
environment, and what needs to change."

—*Bloomberg CityLab*

Takes readers on a journey underground to the
meandering pipes and waterways underneath us where
waste ferments and disease percolates. The oft-forgotten
and hidden-but-so-necessary infrastructure below us
has deep implications for urbanization, public health,
infrastructure, ecology, and sustainability, not to
mention our future."

—*Architect's Newspaper*

Recipe

 Fascinating. . . . [Bloom] explains how recipes unite us, contain lessons about hospitality, and can be a signature as individual as fingerprints."

—*Globe and Mail*

 Recipe celebrates the complications and contradictions, the serious and play, the bounty and scarcity, represented by the simple instructions that put food on the table.."

—Karen Babine, author of *All the Wild Hungers: A Season of Cooking and Cancer and Water and What We Know: Following the Roots of a Northern Life*